A HAMLYN POINTER BOOK

ROCKETS
and
MISSILES

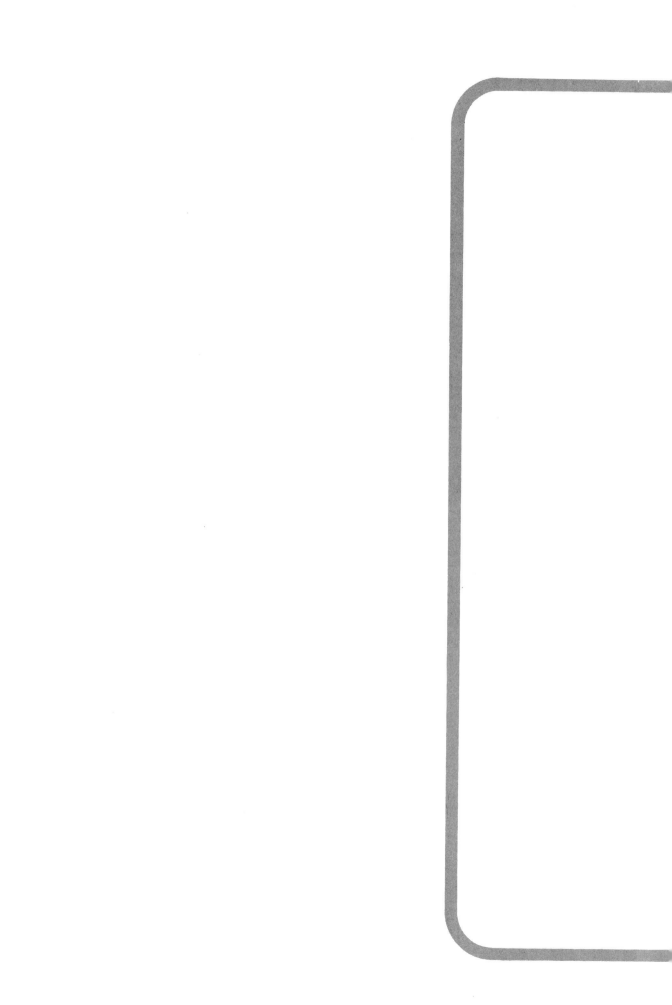

 A HAMLYN POINTER BOOK

ROCKETS and MISSILES

By David Mondey

Illustrated by Gordon Davies

HAMLYN
LONDON · NEW YORK · SYDNEY · TORONTO

For my two grandsons, Christian and Paul.
I trust they may live long enough
to see man's wisdom and technology
achieve lasting world peace.

The illustrations in this book have been
selected from the Hamlyn all-colour paperback
ROCKETS AND MISSILES by John W. R. Taylor

First published 1971
Second impression 1972
Published by The Hamlyn Publishing Group Limited
London · New York · Sydney · Toronto
Hamlyn House, Feltham, Middlesex, England
© Copyright The Hamlyn Publishing Group Limited 1971
ISBN 0 600 30079 X
Printed by Officine Grafiche Arnoldo Mondadori,
Verona, Italy.

contents

Page

BIRTH OF
THE ROCKET

We shall never know who invented the rocket, but it is easy to guess how it happened. The Chinese began using firework crackers more than 2,000 years ago to celebrate weddings, births and religious festivals. These fire-crackers usually consisted of a section of bamboo cane into which a gunpowder mixture was packed tightly, exploding with a satisfying bang soon after the fuse was lit. One day, instead of exploding, a fire-cracker of this kind may have burned slowly at one end – rather like a squib – and begun streaking along the ground.

Before long, somebody must have had the bright idea of using the rocket as a fire-bomb. Tied to an arrow, the tail-feathers would keep it on a straight course. When it was found that the feathers made no difference they were left off. The resulting rocket

Right: In the early 19th century most European armies were using military rockets. The illustration shows Austrian troops firing stick rockets.

Left: Congreve rockets being fired from the British sloop *Erebus* against Fort McHenry, Baltimore, in 1812. The resulting fires caused Francis Scott Key to write a verse about the "rocket's red glare", which became part of America's national anthem.

must have looked like one that you or I might buy to launch on a celebration day.

By the thirteenth century weapons of this kind were used widely by the Chinese. Sometimes they were fired in huge salvoes from cylinders or boxes that could hold as many as a hundred rockets, often with poison smeared on their tips. They gave them strange names, like "long-snake-crush-enemy" or "leopard-herd-rush-across-field", but their effect was often more frightening than destructive. However, Kiang-chin, governor of the town of K'ai-fung-fu, managed to keep at least 30,000 Mongol invaders at bay for many months by using such simple rockets to break up their repeated assaults.

When, in their turn, the Mongols used them during their capture of Baghdad in 1258, and against Japan in 1274, they could not possibly have guessed that

almost 700 years later a peaceful use of rockets would put Men on the Moon.

HOW A ROCKET WORKS

A modern long-range military rocket, or the kind used to send a spacecraft to the Moon, is made from materials which must be light in weight but tremendously strong, and able to withstand very high temperatures without bending, burning or melting. The propellant, the fuel that is burned in the rocket, must produce enormous power, and the system that guides it must ensure that it will reach its target, however great the distance.

Nearly 300 years ago the British scientist, Sir Isaac Newton, stated as one of his famous laws of

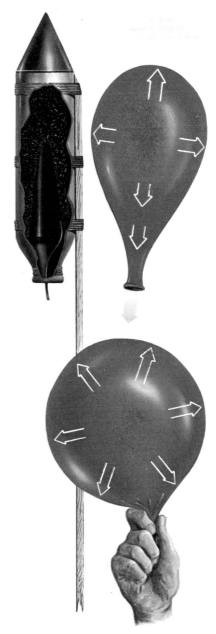

Above: If you blow up a balloon it grows round, because the air inside exerts the same force in every direction. If you release the neck air escapes, creating an unbalanced condition. Air within the balloon presses on the rubber skin (Newton's "action") except at the low-pressure point at the neck and the balloon flies away in the opposite direction (Newton's "reaction"). A rocket works in the same way, hot gases replacing the air in the balloon.

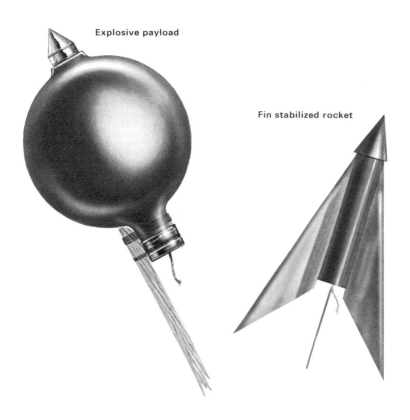

Explosive payload

Fin stabilized rocket

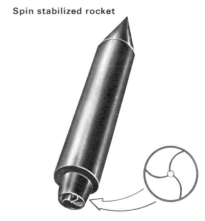

Spin stabilized rocket

Rear end showing vanes
designed to spin rocket

Above: Such rockets were so inaccurate they had to be launched in large numbers to make sure that some of them hit the target. The Frenchman, Frezier, made some improvement in accuracy by adding metal fins, similar to those of an arrow or dart. An Englishman, William Hale, found the best solution was to make the rocket spin as it travelled through the air. He achieved this by putting a series of small vanes in the rocket's efflux (stream of exhaust gases) and a ring of small secondary nozzles through which some of the exhaust gases could escape. This technique is known now as spin-stabilization.

Right: An Englishman, Henry Trengrouse, first used rockets to rescue sailors from inshore wrecks. The rocket which he fired across the ship had a light line with a heavy rope attached to it. When this line fell on the ship the sailors could haul on board the heavy rope, along which they could climb to safety.

motion that "action and reaction are equal and opposite". It sounds rather difficult, but it means that if you try to jump to the shore from a small rowing boat you may get a soaking, because the effort that launches you towards the bank also pushes the boat farther away from it.

The force which propels you towards the bank (the "action") is matched by an equal force moving the boat in the opposite direction (the "reaction").

A rocket works in the same way as the balloon illustrated on page 7. Its casing is filled with materials that burn easily and produce a large volume of hot gas. This is ejected from the tail of the rocket, which moves away in the opposite direction to the escaping, or exhaust gases.

If you think about this carefully you will realize that the escaping gases do not have to push against anything to make the rocket move. This means that it can fly in a vacuum, a space where no air exists. In fact, it works even better under these conditions, for there is no air resistance helping to stop the rocket

Right: Trengrouse's rockets had little range, especially if launched into a gale. In 1855 Lt Col R. A. Boxer made a two-stage rocket, soon to equip all British lifeboat and coastguard stations.

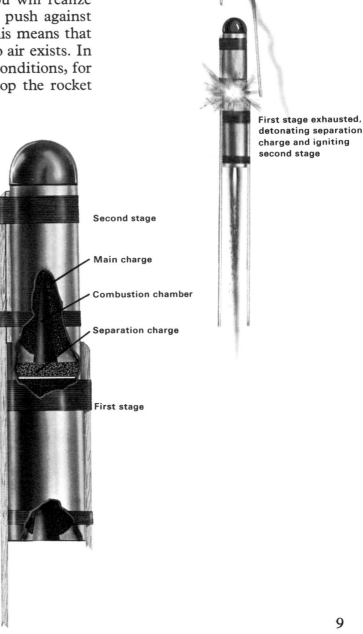

Second stage at maximum thrust

First stage falling away

First stage exhausted, detonating separation charge and igniting second stage

Second stage

Main charge

Combustion chamber

Separation charge

First stage

from moving forward, and no natural air pressure (atmospheric pressure) to reduce the speed at which the burning gases escape.

ROCKETS BECOME MORE WARLIKE

The rockets which the Mongols fired on Baghdad and Japan were soon copied by other nations, but by the end of the seventeenth century France led the world in rocket development. By that time, however, improvements in cannon and small arms suggested that the life of the military rocket was at an end.

But Britain decided to use rockets against the French and Col (later Sir) William Congreve began the development of incendiary and case-shot rockets. Lead shot was discharged in all directions to kill or injure the enemy. These early artillery rockets were so inaccurate they had to be launched in very large numbers to make sure that at least some of them hit the target.

FATHER OF SPACE FLIGHT

Konstantin Eduardovich Tsiolkowsky was born in the small town of Izhevskoye in Russia. He came from a humble family, but worked hard to educate himself and by the age of twenty-one became a schoolmaster. Almost twenty years later he first proposed the use of liquid propellants to power a rocket engine. He even suggested the use of liquid oxygen and liquid hydrogen, fuels that are used to power many modern rockets. He also designed what he called a passenger rocket train to carry men on their first journeys into space.

Tsiolkowsky died on 19 September 1935, always to be remembered as the true father of space flight.

Left: The American, Robert Goddard, was the first man to put advanced rocket theory into practice, and began by making small military rockets for the U.S. armed forces. His first liquid-propellant rocket engine ran successfully on a test bench in 1923 and three years later he launched the very first rocket of this type at Auburn, Massachusetts. He used "The Hearse" to tow his rockets to the launch site.

Below: (1) The Ente glider and (2) von Opel's rocket glider at speed.

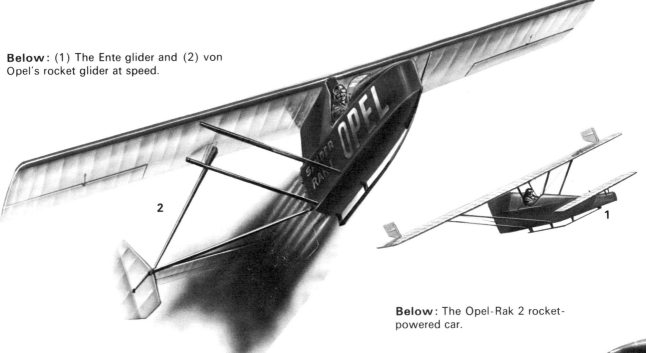

Below: The Opel-Rak 2 rocket-powered car.

IMPORTANT FIRST STEPS IN AMERICA

Robert Goddard, born at Worcester, Massachusetts on 5 October 1882, is remembered as a pioneer of experimental rocketry. He turned the theories of men like Tsiolkowsky into fact. He worked mainly on solid-propellant rockets until 1920 when he began to study seriously how to guide them with gyroscopes and use the far greater energy of liquid-propellants.

Real success came in 1935 when his rockets climbed to 2,286 m and flew at speeds up to 1,127 km/h. Until his death in 1945, he persevered at an amazing independent development programme.

GERMANY SETS THE PACE

After the First World War, Germany's men turned to gliders and rockets as an outlet for their ambitions.

Early experiments soon made headline news and car manufacturer Fritz von Opel used solid-propellant rockets to power two racing cars. The most successful was Opel-Rak 2 which clocked 201 km/h in 1928.

Rockets were soon used to power many experimental vehicles, including aircraft. First to fly successfully was the Ente sailplane, powered by two rockets. More exciting was von Opel's glider, which he flew to a speed of 153 km/h in September 1928.

VfR to V-2

Early rocket experiments in Germany soon attracted a group of young men who were aware that more advanced research was necessary if the aims of their society, the VfR (Society for Space Travel), were to be realized. A leading member of the VfR was a young student, Wernher von Braun, and though he and his fellow members were interested only in the pos-

Right: Rocket-firing Typhoons of the R.A.F. attacking Nazi tanks.

sibilities of space flight, the rockets they made led eventually to new and lethal weapons of war.

They built first a small rocket (Mirak 1) powered by liquid oxygen and gasoline. It and its successor were both destroyed when their oxygen tanks burst. Then, in 1931, they began the design of a new rocket in which the rocket engine was cooled by water stored in its double-skin walls. By August 1931, improved models of this type, known as Repulsor 4, were able to climb to a height of 1,600 m and were then recovered by parachute.

In 1934 the Nazi regime brought an end to private rocket experiments and von Braun was soon working for the German army, this time on military rockets. Under the leadership of Capt. Walter Dornberger and von Braun, the army began building two liquid-propellant rockets. Then, in 1937, there came a move to a new and secret base at Peenemünde on the Baltic coast. Before the Second World War had begun

Above left: the German Me 163 and **Above:** a Japanese Ohka, both rocket fighters of the Second World War.

Above: Germany's V-1 flying bomb.
Right: the German A-3 rocket of 1939

their latest rocket – the A-3 – which used liquid oxygen and alcohol as its propellants, had reached a record height of 12 km. From this rocket evolved a larger version known originally as the A-4, but remembered better as the V-2 (*Vergeltungswaffen* – reprisal weapon). This had been tested as early as 3 October 1942, when it reached a height of 80 km and covered a range of 193 km.

ROCKETS IN THE SECOND WORLD WAR

Most advanced of all rockets used in the Second World War was the V-2, which was more than 14 m in length, and weighed 12,247 kg, of which 1,016 kg consisted of high-explosive packed into its warhead. It was a completely new and terrifying weapon, mainly because it was travelling faster than the speed of sound and impacted on its target without any warning. After detonation of the warhead the thunderous roar of its approach – not unlike the sound of an express train – could be heard. Perhaps

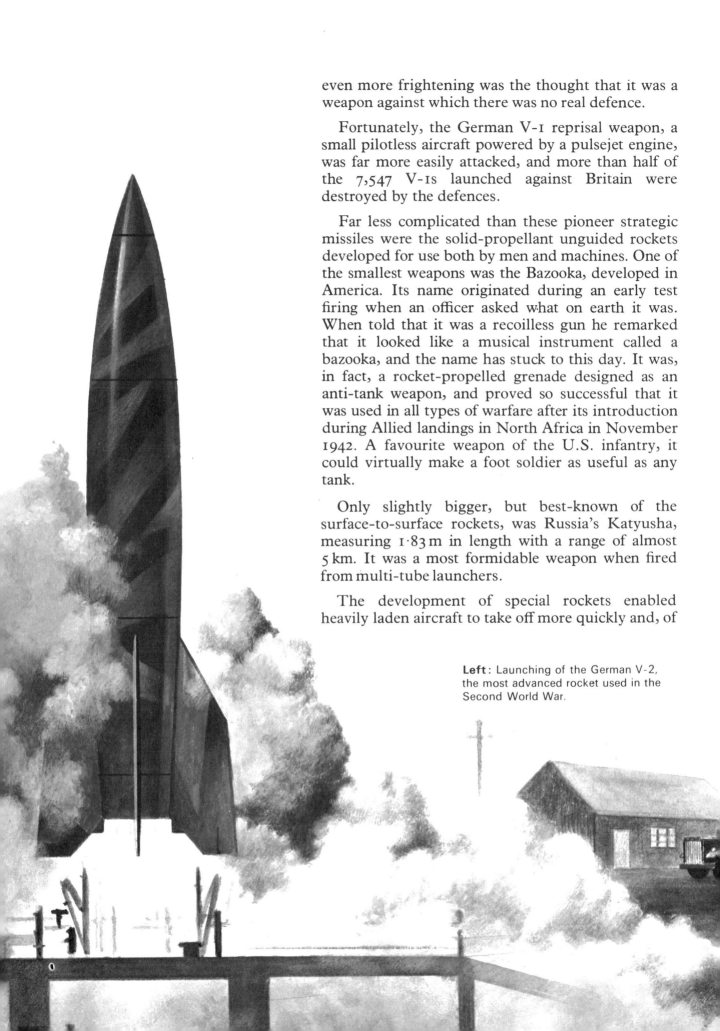

even more frightening was the thought that it was a weapon against which there was no real defence.

Fortunately, the German V-1 reprisal weapon, a small pilotless aircraft powered by a pulsejet engine, was far more easily attacked, and more than half of the 7,547 V-1s launched against Britain were destroyed by the defences.

Far less complicated than these pioneer strategic missiles were the solid-propellant unguided rockets developed for use both by men and machines. One of the smallest weapons was the Bazooka, developed in America. Its name originated during an early test firing when an officer asked what on earth it was. When told that it was a recoilless gun he remarked that it looked like a musical instrument called a bazooka, and the name has stuck to this day. It was, in fact, a rocket-propelled grenade designed as an anti-tank weapon, and proved so successful that it was used in all types of warfare after its introduction during Allied landings in North Africa in November 1942. A favourite weapon of the U.S. infantry, it could virtually make a foot soldier as useful as any tank.

Only slightly bigger, but best-known of the surface-to-surface rockets, was Russia's Katyusha, measuring 1·83 m in length with a range of almost 5 km. It was a most formidable weapon when fired from multi-tube launchers.

The development of special rockets enabled heavily laden aircraft to take off more quickly and, of

Left: Launching of the German V-2, the most advanced rocket used in the Second World War.

course, rockets armed many fighter aircraft of all combatant nations. Most successful was the R.A.F.'s Typhoon which could carry four 27 kg rockets under each wing. In the picture on page 13 a squadron of Typhoons is shown attacking German armoured vehicles. Whole divisions of these were destroyed in this way following the Allied landings in France in June 1944.

GERMAN SECRET WEAPONS

The research and development which had produced the successful V-1 and V-2 *Vergeltungswaffen* had aided and encouraged the design of several evolutionary weapons. Some of them did not enter production; one of these was the rocket-powered Ba 349 Natter that was intended to be launched vertically from a ramp to make a single attack with rocket weapons on Allied bomber squadrons. It was followed by a number of other surface-to-air (i.e. anti-aircraft) missiles such as Enzian, a ramp-launched design based on the Me 163 fighter; Wasserfall, a radio-controlled weapon; Feuerlilie, an experimental missile of the 1943–44 period; and Schmetterling, which was put into production too late to be used in action.

Of those which were produced, most successful were the Ruhrstahl SD 1400X free-falling armour-piercing bomb and the Henschel Hs 293 rocket-propelled bomb.

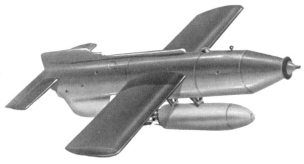

Above: the Hs 293 radio-controlled rocket-powered bomb.

Above: the Ba 349 Natter interceptor, to be launched vertically by rocket engines.

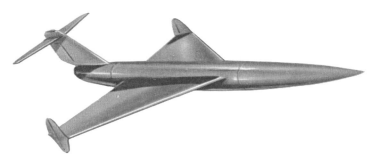

Above: Feuerlilie and **Right**: the radio-controlled Wasserfall, both anti-aircraft missile projects.

THE DEVELOPMENT OF POST-WAR MISSILES

In talking about the V-2 rocket and other advanced projects that were developed during the Second World War, we have taken an immense jump from the simple two-stage stick rocket of Colonel Boxer. In fact, we have taken far too big a jump, for we have quite ignored how rockets were able gradually to gain in altitude and range and, equally important, how they could be guided to the desired target.

The simple firework rocket that you or I can buy and launch from our garden relies upon the rocket's stick to keep it travelling in a straight line. We can aim it very roughly in the direction we wish it to travel but it is diverted easily from the intended flight path by even a moderate breeze. For us, altitude is governed largely by how much money we have to spend. If we buy a lot of small rockets we must be satisfied to see them climb to a low altitude. If we spend all our money on one super big rocket then we shall certainly see it climb high into the night sky.

INCREASING HEIGHT AND RANGE

An ordinary firework rocket will usually consist of a simple tube of cardboard into which the propellant charge is packed, and this is then fixed to a small stick. The top of the tube is quite blunt and the opposite end of the tube is covered only by the touch-paper or fuse.

Above: Honest John artillery rockets on their mobile launchers. The earliest American rocket of this class, it could be fired by a crew of six men and was able to carry its warhead for more than 19 km. Immediately after leaving its launcher it is spun by a number of small rockets placed behind the bulbous warhead and the spin-stabilization is then maintained by the canted tail-fins. Honest John is capable of causing such a large area of damage that a more complex guidance system is not needed.

Right: A Russian FROG (Free Rocket Over Ground) artillery rocket on its amphibious — land or water traversing — transporter. The Soviets have a family of FROGs with ranges varying from 24 to 48 km, carrying either high-explosive or nuclear warheads. Like Honest John and Littlejohn, they rely for their guidance upon the spin-stabilization technique, and are powered by single- or two-stage solid-propellant rockets.

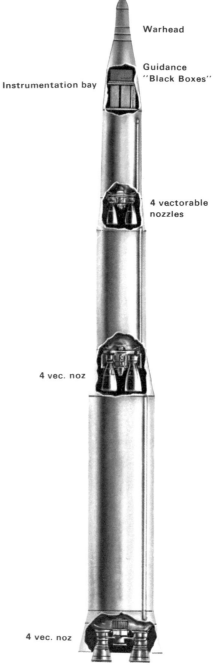

Warhead

Guidance "Black Boxes"

Instrumentation bay

4 vectorable nozzles

4 vec. noz

4 vec. noz

An expensive firework rocket will be pointed at the top – streamlined – to enable it to pass more easily through the air; the bottom of the tube will have a small hole under the fuse, so that the escaping gases have to travel much faster. This narrowing-down of the exhaust nozzle is called a venturi and, as a rough guide, if we design this to double the speed of the exhaust gases we also double the speed of the rocket.

The most simple military rockets are much like our firework rocket, but they dispense with the stick. The casing of the rocket which contains the propellant has metal fins at its base and this serves to keep it on course. Here the similarity ends, for at the head of the military rocket is the warhead, packed with high-explosive, and the charge which propels it is usually a solid-propellant, moulded with a star-shaped hole extending the length of the charge. This shape – known as a cruciform – ensures that the greatest possible surface area is burning at the same time, and thus producing the maximum volume of gas to hurl the rocket through the air.

Above: America's Minuteman missile, which is powered by solid-propellant motors, is seen in cut-away form to show the rocket chambers of its three stages and the guidance "black boxes" beneath the warhead.

LIQUID-PROPELLANTS

Why, then, are liquid-propellants chosen for so many of the big rockets? The reason is that they produce far more energy in the form of fast-moving exhaust gases than does the old-fashioned gunpowder type solid-propellant.

The snag is that they add enormously to the rocket's complexity. The difficult-to-handle liquids have to be contained in special tanks, and pumps, valves and metering systems are needed to control the flow of the liquids and inject very precise quantities of them into the combustion chamber.

STEERING THE ROCKET

The most simple means of steering the rocket to its target is by putting movable vanes – which work like a ship's rudder – in the rocket's efflux. Alternatively, the nozzle through which the exhaust gases are discharged can be moved. This is known as vectored thrust. Unfortunately, such devices will not operate without a control system, and this adds both to the weight and complexity of a modern missile.

Right: America's Corporal rocket was guided by radio command. How such a system is used to direct an anti-aircraft missile to its target is shown in the diagram. Two separate radars track missile and bomber, and a computer uses the radar information to steer the missile to the bomber by radio signals.

Above: A Mace-A, its wings folded for transit, on its multi-wheeled launch trailer, hauled by a Teracruzer tractor. The huge tyres of both vehicles have their pressures adjusted automatically to suit the ground surface.

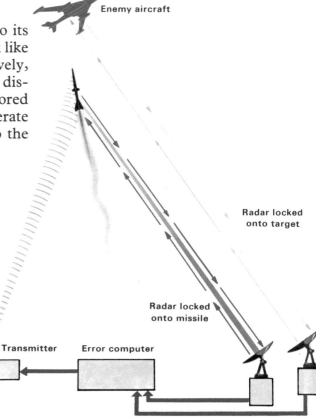

Enemy aircraft

Radar locked onto target

Radar locked onto missile

Transmitter   Error computer

Above: Russia's and in fact the world's first intermediate-range ballistic missile (IRBM), was given the NATO code name "Shyster". It had a range of 1,200 km.

Above: The first big surface-to-surface missiles developed in America were Redstone and the smaller Corporal.

I am sure you have seen a model aeroplane being flown under radio-control, and this method is used to guide many short-range rockets. The real complications arise when an intercontinental ballistic missile (ICBM) has to be guided when it is not possible for anyone to visually monitor its flight path and keep it on course.

To resolve this sort of problem, scientists and engineers have designed systems that enable a rocket's control circuits to keep it on course over very long ranges. This degree of automation, however, makes a modern missile a most costly weapon.

Armies throughout the world continue to use simple unguided solid-propellant rockets like the wartime Katyusha and Bazooka. Of course, much larger types have been built, and the availability of a nuclear – atomic – warhead meant that many early weapons of short-range could remain unguided as the explosion of such a missile would create devastation over so large an area that there was no need for it to be exactly on target.

EARLY FLYING-BOMBS

Years of experience with winged aircraft caused the U.S. Air Force to use such vehicles as the basis of its earliest missiles. First into service in 1955 was Matador, with a range of 1,046 km. It was followed by the more highly developed Mace-A and Mace-B.

But these were fairly slow weapons which stood a fair chance of being destroyed by an enemy's defences. Both America and Russia were anxious to develop very long-range missiles based on the V-2 against which, if you remember, there was no

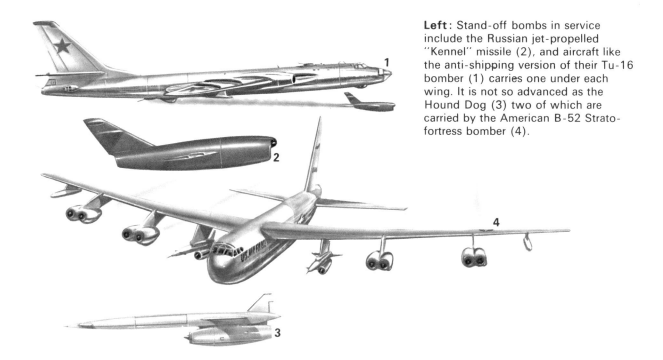

Left: Stand-off bombs in service include the Russian jet-propelled "Kennel" missile (2), and aircraft like the anti-shipping version of their Tu-16 bomber (1) carries one under each wing. It is not so advanced as the Hound Dog (3) two of which are carried by the American B-52 Strato-fortress bomber (4).

Right: Since the end of the Second World War no new major war has developed and this is because the more powerful nations have had nuclear weapons available which could create such terrible devastation that the likelihood of a Third World War is very remote. The threat of massive counter-attack is enough to deter – stop – a nation from starting a nuclear war. From this we see the meaning of deterrent power. Great Britain has maintained such power by her superb Vulcan bomber able to carry a Blue Steel H-bomb missile.

defence. As a result both nations spent huge sums of money to build such weapons.

Air-launched air-to-surface missiles are not new. In the Second World War the German *Luftwaffe* pioneered the idea by launching V-1 flying-bombs from Heinkel He 111 bombers. By carrying the V-1 beneath an aircraft its range could be greatly extended; and it meant also that an attack could be made from almost any point of the compass, thus making the missile far more difficult to intercept.

Of even greater importance today is the fact that, by using self-propelled missiles, the launching aircraft need not approach too close to a heavily defended target. This has extended considerably the useful life of conventional bomber aircraft.

These missiles are often called stand-off bombs, since they allow the launch plane to "stand-off" at a safe distance from the target. Typical of this type is

the jet-powered Hound Dog, carried by America's B-52 Stratofortresses, with a range of more than 965 km and a speed of 2,090 km/h.

CONFUSING THE DEFENCES

The development of advanced anti-aircraft missiles and defence systems, which are described later in this book, have made the task of the attacking aircraft or missile a very difficult one. It is no longer possible for an aircraft to rely upon high altitude to evade anti-aircraft fire or upon high speed to outpace defending fighters.

Instead, a great deal of research has been carried out to put into service special missiles intended to confuse or destroy an enemy's radar system, which is the keystone of his defence. Without radar a defender cannot "see" an attack developing in sufficient time to direct missiles or fighters to intercept it.

An early defence missile carried by American bombers was the jet-powered Quail. When released it would fly on a carefully planned course and, while doing so, send out signals to either jam the enemy's radar system or give an image on the radar screen that could not be distinguished from the B-52 bomber that had launched it.

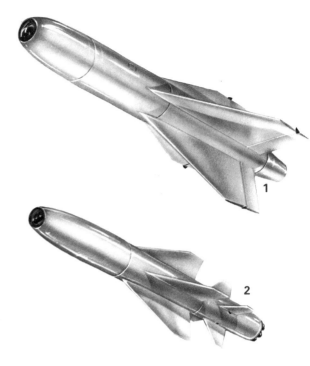

Above: Two air-to-air surface missiles. Walleye (1) and Martel (2) each have a glass eye in their nose. Behind this a TV camera which, once it has focussed on the target, homes the missile on to it automatically.
Below: Confusing an enemy's radar defence is the job of the unique Quail decoy missile.

Below: The diagram shows the French AS 12 air-to-surface missile being controlled by a TCA (*Télécommande Automatique*) guidance system. The operator centres the target in an optical sight and an infra-red device detects heat from flares on the missile. The angle of its flight path in relation to the operator's line of sight is worked out by a computer, which transmits signals along two fine wires, which unwind as the weapon streaks to its target.

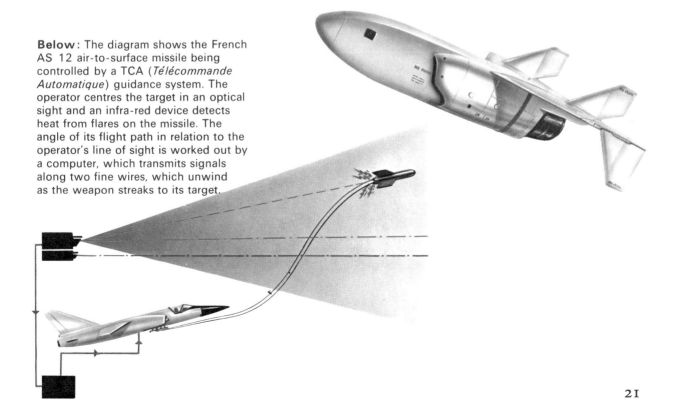

Left: One infantryman can fire the British Vigilant wire-guided anti-tank weapon, which has a maximum range of about 1,600 m and is able to pierce armour plate more than 5·58 cm in thickness.

Vigilant is a lightweight weapon, one-man portable. Guidance is by an optical line-of-sight command control system, the operator watching the flight of the missile towards the target through an optical sight. A flare is provided at the rear of Vigilant to make it easier for him to see the weapon as it streaks to the target at some 560 km/h.

ANTI-TANK MISSILES

Special guided missiles have been developed for launch against heavily armoured vehicles like tanks. So powerful are some of these weapons that they can penetrate armour plate 61 cm thick at short-range.

The missile's task is to knock out a tank by a direct hit, but this ability would be of little use on the battlefield unless the weapon could be fired without delay, directed accurately to its target and be handled by a minimum number of men. America's wartime Bazooka had two of these three desirable characteristics, but modern warfare makes guidance essential. One of the more recent U.S. anti-tank missiles is known as TOW, which stands for Tube-launched, Optically-tracked and Wire-guided.

TOW has a special two-stage solid-propellant motor, the first stage firing to propel the missile from the launcher. The missile then coasts for a short period to ensure safety for the operator, after which the second stage ignites. It is guided by a single operator who centres the target in a special sight, movement of which signals corrections to the missile.

Below: The illustration shows the British Vigilant anti-tank weapon leaving its transportable launcher, which is easily prepared to fire the missile.

An interesting feature of Vigilant is its ability to be used against close-range targets, achieved by using special control surfaces on the weapon which allow it to make very tight turns. After practice on a training device, known as a simulator, the average soldier can hit a moving target first time.

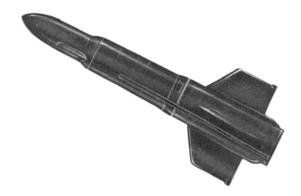

SOVIET ANTI-TANK MISSILES

Russia and her Allies have developed anti-tank weapons which are very similar to those designed in the Western hemisphere. This is not surprising since they are intended to carry out the same task and, like their Western counterparts, are powered mainly by solid-propellants and wire-guided.

This system of wire-guidance may, at first sight, seem rather clumsy, and I expect you have wondered whether the wires become tangled or break. In fact it is a very practical system. The use of wire to carry guidance signals to the missile is far less complicated than providing a radio transmitter on the ground and a receiver and complex relays in the missile. This makes the complete anti-tank system smaller, and reduces the number of personnel needed to carry, service and operate its components.

Russian anti-tank weapons are particularly interesting for the clever way in which they are carried on their launch vehicles. The earliest of which we had detailed knowledge has the NATO code name "Snapper", examples of which were captured from the Egyptian army by Israeli forces during the Sinai campaign, in June 1967. "Snapper" is guided by an operator who has special binoculars with which to sight the target. He controls the missile by a small joystick, the resulting guidance signals passing through the trailing wires.

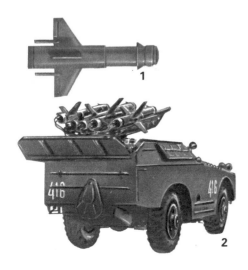

Right: A "Styx" surface-to-surface missile being launched from a Komar-class patrol boat of the Soviet navy.

This type of weapon is standard on Komar- and Osa-class vessels, and in general appearance is very much like a small delta-wing aeroplane. It is boosted at launch by a large solid-propellant motor that is dropped after take-off, the missile cruising to its target powered by an internal rocket motor.

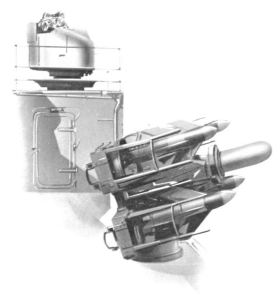

Above: The British Royal Navy's Seacat surface-to-air missile is part of a complete weapon system designed to deal with low-flying aircraft or missiles like "Styx".

Seacat is basically a short-range weapon powered by a two-stage solid-propellant motor. It is controlled by a Mk 20 director unit, one operator turning the director, the other tracking the target through binoculars and guiding the missile by a small joystick.

MISSILES GO TO SEA

Large naval craft were once considered a most formidable weapon: they could cruise the oceans of the world, and were easily able to use their heavy guns against an enemy target many thousands of miles from their home waters. The advent of the aeroplane made their task more hazardous, but a combination of ship and aeroplane known as an aircraft carrier – virtually a floating aerodrome – seemed once again to restore naval prestige in the Second World War.

The post-war development of missiles, and in particular those for use at sea, means that it is now possible for quite small vessels to pack the sort of punch that once could be delivered only by large and vulnerable battleships.

This point is well demonstrated by an action which took place on 21 October 1967 when "Styx" surface-to-surface missiles launched by an Egyptian patrol boat, hit and sank the Israeli destroyer *Eilat* some 19 km off-shore. At the time of the attack the two countries were not officially at war, and it seems likely that the crew of the *Eilat* were quite unprepared, and so were unable to take any evasive action.

The missiles had been launched from Osa-class fast patrol boats, both missiles and vessels having been supplied to the Egyptians by Russia.

Despite the fact that armies and air forces throughout the world switched quickly to missiles for short-range bombardment, at first only the Russian navy replaced shipboard guns by missiles like "Styx".

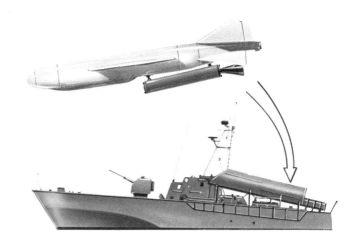

Right: Two "Styx" missiles are housed in individual hangars – from which they are launched – one on each side of a Russian Komar-class fast patrol boat. The upper illustration gives a side view of "Styx", showing clearly the booster rocket used for launching.

Above: The U.S. Navy's Talos missile mounted on its two-round launcher. An early naval missile for surface-to-air or surface-to-surface use, it uses beam-riding guidance. A narrow beam of radio signals is directed at the target, and the missile flies along this path, kept in the radio beam by its own equipment. It is launched by a solid-propellant booster, but cruises to the target powered by a ramjet sustainer motor.

However, there now seems to be every sign that all this has changed. A number of highly efficient new short-range surface-to-surface naval missiles have been developed by several countries and are now in the process of being tested by their respective navies.

Of course, it should be understood that naval vessels have carried long-range bombardment and anti-aircraft missiles for a considerable time: it is the development of short-range weapons to replace the conventional heavy guns that has taken rather longer to evolve.

This is quite understandable; a battleship's heavy guns have proved effective for very many years, and their replacement by missiles had to wait until scientists and engineers had designed sighting, guidance and control equipment that would react quickly and reliably in all weathers.

Right: Perhaps the most simple of the many short-range surface-to-surface missiles being developed for Naval use is the French SS 12M, seen here being used to arm a fast patrol boat. Solid-propellant powered and wire-guided, it can be launched without delay against targets up to 5·6 km distant. The missiles are usually carried on a lightweight launcher which is gyro-stabilized to compensate for ship movement.

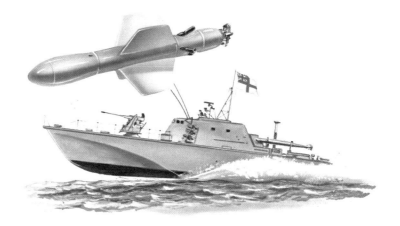

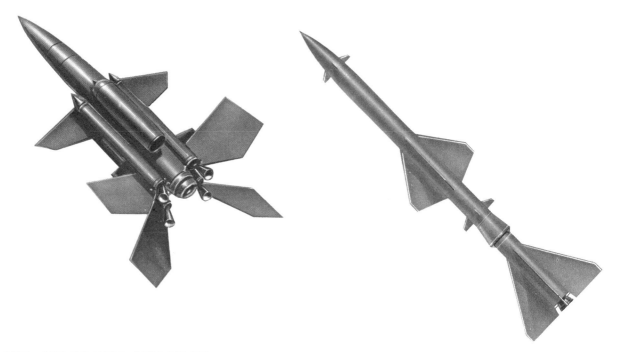

ANTI-AIRCRAFT MISSILES

At the end of the Second World War two new inventions combined into one deadly weapon posed entirely new defence problems. These were the jet-bomber, able to fly at heights of 15,000 m, and the atomic bomb it could carry to any part of the world.

Until this moment arrived, air forces armed with high-speed interceptor aircraft had been able to deal with bombers even if a few of the bombers had always managed to reach the target. The immense area of devastation caused by the explosion of an atomic bomb meant that no longer could a single bomber be allowed to reach and attack its target.

The answer to the problem appeared to be the development of long-range surface-to-air guided missiles, working in partnership with fighter aircraft armed with air-to-air missiles.

Perhaps the most difficult part of the task was to

Above left: Britain's Bloodhound anti-aircraft missile for defence against targets flying below 300 m. Powered by two ramjet engines, it has semi-active homing guidance. The target is illuminated by ground radar, causing radiation to be reflected from it on to which the missile homes.

Above: Russia's "Guideline" anti-aircraft missile for defence against high-altitude targets. It has been used for some time in the Vietnam War.

Right: America's first operational surface-to-air missile was Nike-Ajax, and three of these weapons are seen on their ramps ready for launch.
   This was a two-stage missile, with a solid-propellant first stage booster and a liquid-propellant second stage. When it was used first to protect American cities it had a range of only 40 km, but was subsequently replaced by Nike-Hercules, with a range of 120 km and a maximum speed of 3,540 km/h.

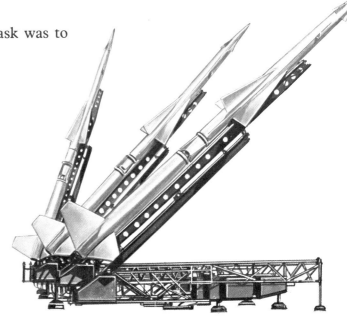

Right: America's Hawk surface-to-air missile was one of the first weapons of the type designed to deal with low-flying bombers: it is shown on a self-propelled launcher that could carry as many as three missiles.

One of the problems in dealing with aircraft that make their attack at low-level is that it is difficult to identify the moving target on the radar screen, due to a clutter of images that are reflected from objects like trees and buildings. Hawk had a special guidance system which was specifically designed to overcome this.

design guidance systems that could track both incoming bomber and defending missile, and guide the latter on a course that would ensure destruction of the bomber long before it reached its target. The earliest American missile of this type was the Boeing Bomarc which, on 23 October 1957, destroyed a flying target more than 160 km from its launch point at a height of 19 km.

DEALING WITH LOW-LEVEL ATTACK

Surface-to-air missiles soon became so effective at high altitudes that attacking bombers had to change their plan of attack. The alternative was to fly fast and low, thus making their detection more difficult. This meant that completely new anti-aircraft weapons had to be devised, for existing guidance systems took time to take over control of the missile and were too slow to deal with aircraft attacking at tree-top height.

Below: (1) in Britain a Bazooka-like anti-aircraft weapon system has been developed for defence against low-flying aircraft: and it can easily be carried and operated by one man. Here its similarity to the Bazooka ends, for it is a far more advanced weapon that can be prepared for action in as little as twenty seconds. Known as Blow-pipe, the whole system weighs less than 18 kg.

Rapier (2) is also for use against low-flying aircraft, and is part of a weapon system that has been developed in Britain. This consists of a launcher-trailer towed by a Land Rover, which also carries the tracker, radio equipment, and four missiles in sealed containers. A radar-tracking system is under development so that Rapier can be used in darkness or poor visibility.

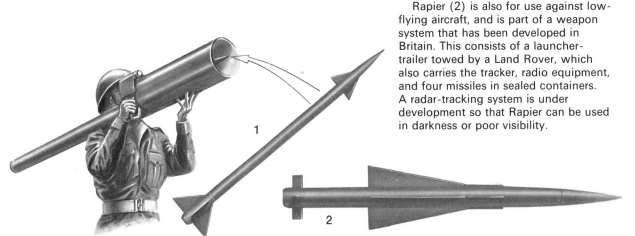

DEFENCE AGAINST MISSILES

You will remember that, when talking about the German V-2 rocket, we said that its most frightening aspect was that there was no means of defence against it. This statement was not strictly correct because by bombing the launch sites it was possible to prevent the rockets being sent on their journey of destruction.

When ICBMs were developed it was soon realized that a policy of dispersal – siting the weapons at long distances from one another – was not

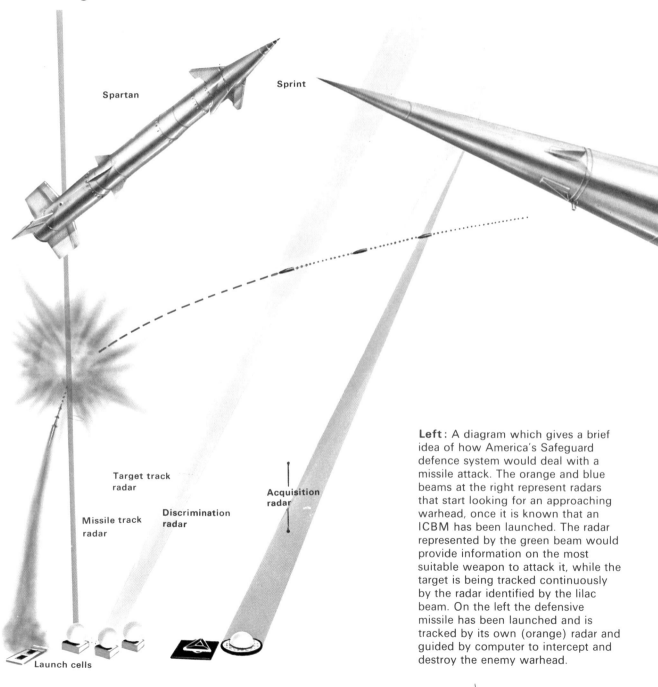

Left: A diagram which gives a brief idea of how America's Safeguard defence system would deal with a missile attack. The orange and blue beams at the right represent radars that start looking for an approaching warhead, once it is known that an ICBM has been launched. The radar represented by the green beam would provide information on the most suitable weapon to attack it, while the target is being tracked continuously by the radar identified by the lilac beam. On the left the defensive missile has been launched and is tracked by its own (orange) radar and guided by computer to intercept and destroy the enemy warhead.

sufficient safeguard. Advanced reconnaissance systems using high-flying aircraft and, as will be described later, special observation satellites, meant that an enemy could learn where the dispersed ICBMs were placed and make sure that, in the event of a war, their first task would be to destroy them. The solution was to house each missile in an underground cell, known as a silo, in which it was quite safe from any conventional aerial attack.

This put the situation back to square one. Since it would not be possible to prevent a missile from being launched, there was no defence against it.

This has meant that both America and Russia have spent gigantic sums of money to develop what are known as anti-missile missiles. You will realize how great a problem it is to provide such a defence system if you consider that an ICBM warhead, a minute target as it re-enters Earth's atmosphere, would be travelling at about 24,000 km/h. You have to know just where it is and be able to launch a missile fast enough to destroy it long before it gets near its target.

As a beginning, America began the construction of huge BMEWS (Ballistic Missile Early-Warning System) radar antennae, to detect and give advance warning of any missiles launched by the Soviet Union. The sites will eventually be replaced by detection satellites, able to give warning of missile launchings anywhere in the world.

Immediately such a warning is received a complex network of detection and communication systems could swing into action to deal with the approaching missile.

A COMPLETE DEFENCE SYSTEM

However costly and complicated, an anti-missile missile system is only part of the complete defensive network that is necessary to protect a nation against all the kinds of attack they may have to cope with.

For some years the U.S.A. and Canada have had a combined defence network, under the control of NORAD (North American Air Defense Command). The task of NORAD is to deal with any attack that may develop, except for one made by ICBMs.

To fulfil this awe-inspiring responsibility, NORAD relies upon information received from radar sites that stretch across Canada and the U.S., as well as from BMEWS radar sites and early-warning aircraft that are kept constantly airborne. These aircraft are designed to detect any missiles, ships and aircraft that slip through the sectors not covered by surface radar.

If the moment ever came to use its defensive aircraft or missiles, NORAD would rely upon an underground network of control posts, known as

Below: The American YF-12A interceptor, capable of a speed of more than 3,220 km/h, and which carries Falcon air-to-air missiles.

Above: An American-built F-4K Phantom in service with the British Royal Navy. This is armed with Sparrow missiles, which are powered by a solid-propellant rocket motor and guided by a semi-active radar homing system. This relies upon a radar transmitter in the nose of the aircraft to illuminate the target, the missile homing on to the reflected signals.

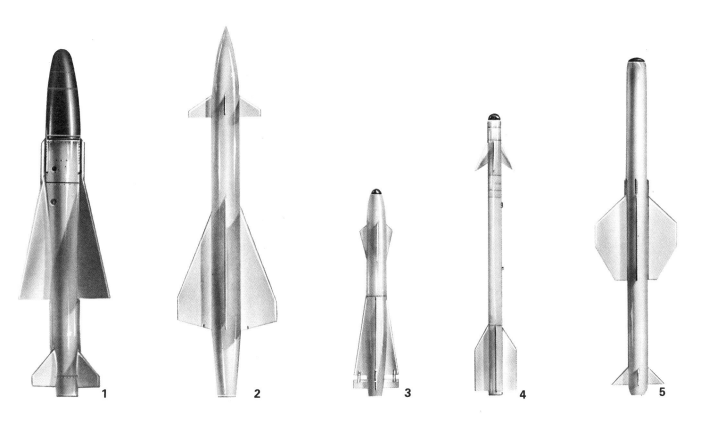

Above: A few of the wide range of air-to-air missiles are illustrated. (1) The French Matra R 530 that arms the Mirage fighter. The version shown relies upon semi-active radar homing, but is available also with infra-red guidance. (2) Code named "Anab", this is Russia's standard air-to-air missile, available in radar and infra-red homing versions. (3) The infra-red homing versions of the American Falcon missile and (4) Sidewinder. (5) The British Red Top infra-red homing missile.

SAGE (Semi-Automatic Ground Environment) to ensure that no potential target was overlooked and that the most suitable weapon, aircraft or missile, was despatched to deal with the threat.

MISSILES FOR AIR COMBAT

At the beginning of the First World War aircraft had not been considered as offensive weapons. Instead, they had been used for observation of enemy positions and troop movements, and to direct the fire of artillery batteries on the ground.

This kind of task proved very valuable. It was not long before the combatants began to consider it necessary to prevent aircraft of the enemy from having free access to the airspace above their territory. This led to the development of a whole range of defensive measures, like anti-aircraft guns, barrage balloons and searchlights.

It led also to the provision of offensive armament for fast, manoeuvrable aircraft able to attack and destroy the reconnaissance aircraft or observation balloons of the enemy.

Air combat in the First World War still retained a little of the chivalrous spirit of the hand-to-hand combat of knights in shining armour. The Second

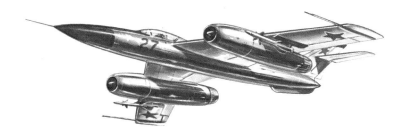

Right: A Yak-28 all-weather fighter of the Soviet Air Force, carrying an "Anab" air-to-air missile under each wing.

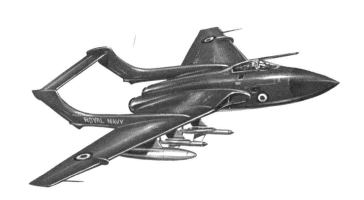

Right: Sea Vixen fighter of the British Royal Navy carrying Firestreak infra-red guided missiles. They can, alternatively, use the more-advanced Red Top. Missiles that rely upon infra-red homing systems are classed as "passive" devices. This means that no guidance signals are sent out either by the missile or the launching aircraft.

Instead, a highly sensitive heat detecting device is located in the nose of the missile, and this is able to "feel" the heat radiated by the engine of an enemy aircraft at very long range and then homes on to the heat source.

Right: A U.S.A.F. F-101B Voodoo fighter is seen carrying two unguided Genie air-to-air rockets, which are armed with a nuclear warhead.

The missile is unguided because its warhead is so powerful that it does not need to hit its target to destroy it. Instead, it is launched and detonated by a special fire-control system carried in the launching aircraft.

Since the missile has a nuclear warhead, special safety devices are absolutely necessary to ensure that it cannot be detonated accidentally. When loaded on the aircraft it remains completely safe until it is made active, and this is done just a few seconds before being fired.

World War changed all this. By then it was appreciated that victory would go to the nation able to use maximum fire-power to the best advantage. The Second World War also gave birth to the jet age.

New airspeeds and altitudes needed new weapons to ensure that, so far as possible, an interceptor aircraft could attack and destroy an enemy bomber at any height under all weather conditions.

Quite naturally, missiles soon became an important part of the interceptor aircraft; but it is not enough to provide an aircraft with an armament of air-to-air missiles, however destructive they may be. Special equipment is needed to fire the weapon at the right moment and guide it to its target, leading to the development of a combination of aircraft and weapons in what is known as a "weapons system".

NO SAFETY IN THE SEA'S DEPTHS

For very many years it was thought that the submarine was a most formidable weapon, mainly because it could hide beneath the surface of the sea and choose the right moment to attack its target. This was certainly the case in the World Wars of the twentieth century, and the successes of German U-boats almost brought Great Britain to her knees.

By the end of the Second World War Germany had submarines that could remain submerged for long periods and post-war development produced nuclear-powered versions that can remain under the water indefinitely, and are as fast as any surface vessel. Soon they were armed with nuclear weapons that could be launched without the vessel surfacing. Fortunately, it is now possible to seek and destroy these undersea craft.

Right: Anti-submarine missiles of the U.S. Navy include Asroc (1). Asroc is a complete weapon system comprising an underwater sonar device to detect the submarine; a fire-control computer; an eight-missile launcher and Asroc itself. This missile has a solid-propellant rocket motor giving a range of up to 9 km.

After detection of a submarine by the sonar device, the computer works out the course, range and speed of the target and turns the missile launcher into firing position. The ship's commander then selects a missile with the most suitable warhead and fires it. After launch the missile follows a ballistic trajectory until a signal from the ship causes it to drop its motor and airframe.

If the payload is a torpedo it is lowered to the water by parachute and then homes automatically on its target: if it is a nuclear depth-charge it sinks and the resulting explosion can "kill" any submarine within a wide radius.

Right: Subroc, shown at (2) is a submarine-to-submarine missile. Launched from a torpedo tube, it is propelled out of the water and then follows a ballistic trajectory to its target where a nuclear depth-charge enters the water to destroy the enemy submarine.

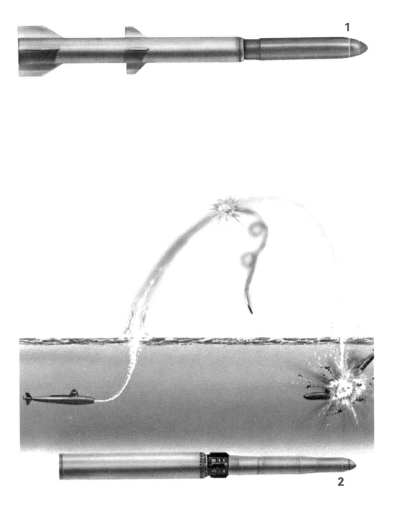

Right: The Malafon anti-submarine missile of the French Navy. It is rather like a small aeroplane built around a torpedo. Launched by two solid-propellant boosters, which drop off after burn-out, Malafon has a maximum range of about 18 km. As seen in the picture on the right a parachute is used to brake the airframe at the right position and the torpedo is ejected into the sea, homing on its target by an acoustic — listening — device which locks on to the sound of the submarine's engines.

THE ULTIMATE WEAPON

We have already mentioned that the development of ICBMs able to carry nuclear warheads was considered as the ultimate weapon; by this is meant a weapon that is so sure and so powerful that there is nothing more deadly. Possession of such a weapon by a single nation would allow it to dominate the rest of the world.

The fully-developed ICBM can be launched to reach any target on the globe, and carries a thermonuclear warhead (Hydrogen bomb) that is capable of wiping out all life from vast areas. However, since ICBMs are possessed by several nations, their effect has been rather to prevent the start of a Third World War.

The reason for this is not too difficult to understand. If one country feels inclined to attack an enemy, it is unlikely to take the risk if it knows that the enemy is able to strike back before being destroyed. There is little point in wiping out one's enemy if, in the process, you also eliminate yourself.

This is the true deterrent policy, and it remains

effective only if it is seen to be so destructive that no nation dare attack another without fear of massive counter-attack.

MAINTAINING THE DETERRENT

We do not know precise details of Russia's deterrent force. We do, have some knowledge of America's defence system.

Atlas and Titan ICBMs were used originally as the long-range striking force of the deterrent, but these have now been phased out of service and replaced by Minuteman ICBMs housed in underground silos. Each flight of ten has its own launch control centre. In the unlikely event of all underground control posts being put out of action, the entire Minuteman force can be launched from airborne control centres. These latter are specially equipped Boeing aircraft.

Above: A Russian ICBM, NATO code name "Sasin", is not thought to have entered military service.

Above: (1) America's Titan 2 which like Atlas (2) is no longer in military use. Both relied upon inertial guidance to take them to targets at least 8,000 km away. This guidance system has highly-sensitive instruments able to detect every slight change in direction of the missile. Information passed to an on-board control system then directs the weapon back on to its pre-determined course. (3) This shows Atlas boosters dropping away at burn-out.

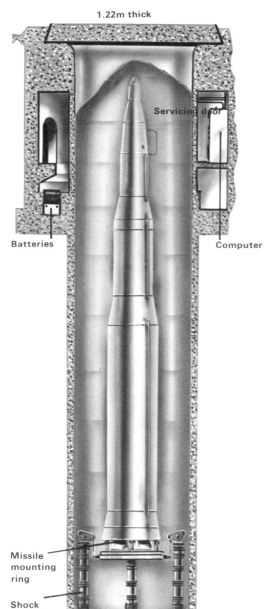

1.22m thick

Servicing door

Batteries

Computer

Missile
mounting
ring

Shock
absorbers

Known as EC-135Cs, at least one of these airborne control posts of the U.S.A.F's Strategic Air Command is always on patrol.

ICBMs FROM UNDER THE SEA

The idea of developing nuclear-powered submarines that could launch ICBMs without surfacing originated because, despite the fact that America's

Above: America's solid-propellant Minuteman ICBM seen housed in its underground silo.

Each silo-launcher has two rooms extending around the silo casing which house equipment.

Minuteman is a three-stage inertially-guided weapon with a maximum speed of about 24,000 km/h at burn-out. There are three versions, Minuteman 1 being phased out as it is replaced by advanced versions, designated Minuteman 2 and 3.

A total of 510 of the latter are expected to be in service by the end of 1973. These carry multiple warheads and have a range of more than 13,000 km.

Above: Polaris A3, which is a more advanced version of the A2, has several new features including solid-propellant rocket motors, an inertial guidance system of reduced size and first and second stage casings of glass-fibre. These changes have increased the range of Polaris to a maximum of 4,630 km.

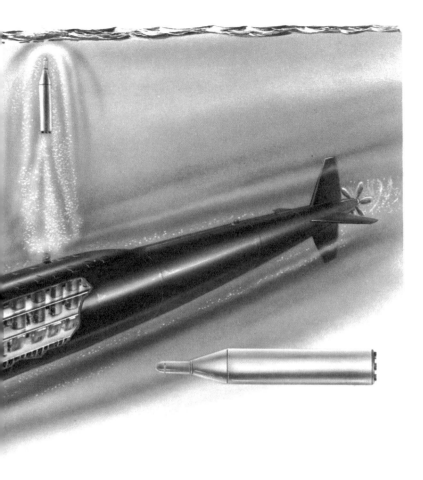

Left: The illustration shows one of America's nuclear submarines, with a section cut away so that you can see how the missiles are contained in vertical launch-tubes. Below the submarine is shown, in greater detail, one of the Polaris A2 missiles.

As a two-stage solid-propellant weapon with inertial guidance, it was found that Polaris could not be launched from beneath the surface of the sea using its first stage motor, as test firings showed this method to be too dangerous. Instead, it is "popped" out of its launch-tube by a small rocket motor, the first stage engine firing when the missile breaks clear of the surface.

Polaris will be replaced eventually by the more advanced Poseidon C3, which can carry double the payload of Polaris. Most important new feature of Poseidon is that it has a warhead which carries what are known as multiple and individually-targeted re-entry vehicles (MIRV). This means that an enemy's defences will have to cope with the problem of more than one warhead entering their airspace at one time. Poseidon entered service with the nuclear submarine fleet in 1971.

Right: The French MSBS inertially-guided missile for underwater launch that is to equip the nuclear-powered submarines of the French Navy.

Minuteman force is housed in underground silos, it is possible that a potential enemy could learn the precise location of each.

A nuclear submarine, able to cruise beneath the surface of the sea for an indefinite period, presents a more difficult target as it can constantly move its position. It is possible to seek and locate submarines underwater but this takes time.

It has been reported that the nuclear submarines of the U.S. Navy each carry 14 missiles, ready for instant launching at any time.

France, too, is equipping each of her nuclear-powered submarines of the SNLE class to carry 16 missiles. This ICBM known as the MSBS (*mer-sol balistique stratégique*) is a two–stage solid-propellant missile with a nuclear warhead containing an inertial guidance system so that it can travel to its target unaided.

ROCKETS INTO SPACE

The success of the German V-2 military rocket led directly to the development of many types of missiles such as those we have read about in the last chapter.

More importantly, however, V-2 represented the first step in the exploration of Earth's atmosphere and of the area beyond, which we call space. German-built rockets were taken to America and Russia following the Second World War and both countries used them to gain experience of rocketry and to carry the first scientific instruments into the upper atmosphere. Unfortunately, V-2 became unstable immediately after burn-out of its rocket engines, limiting the useful data that it could radio back to Earth. Also, the supply of V-2s was limited, leading to development of the first research rockets.

In America the Aerobee, developed from the Corporal rocket illustrated on page 19, became the first of a vast range of what are known as sounding rockets, used throughout the world today as research tools. Aerobee, a simple liquid-propellant rocket launched by a solid-propellant booster, could climb to about 120 km. It carried instruments to radio back to Earth information of vital importance to scientists, whose aim was not only to learn all they could about Earth's atmosphere, but to pave the way to exploration of space itself.

It was followed by a more ambitious rocket developed for the U.S. Naval Research Laboratory. At its launch, on 3 May 1949 this rocket, named Viking, reached a height of 80 km.

Above: The instrument package container of Russia's A-2 rocket. The petal-like fins at the rear act as brakes to stabilize it before its parachute opens: the corrugated nose cone forms a shock-absorber at the moment of landing.

Left: The nose section of Russia's A-3 geophysical rocket, which has carried a payload of 1,700 kg to a height of 450 km. This payload is carried in the 6 m-long nose section which has five separate compartments. The first contains instruments to study the ionosphere, the second contains equipment which carries out biological experiments, while the third houses batteries and an infra-red detector. The two final sections hold recovery parachutes and stabilization and braking mechanisms to ensure the instrument payload is landed without damage.

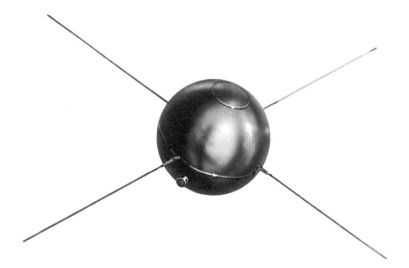

Left: America's Vanguard satellite. Vanguard 1 made a successful first flight on 23 October 1957, but numbers 2 and 3 were failures. Before number 4 was launched Sputnik 2 was orbiting Earth with Laika aboard.

Russian scientists and engineers, like their counterparts in America began experimentation with the V-2 rockets they had taken from Germany. Their progress with large sounding rockets was initially more rapid than that in America, and as early as 1949 they had carried out a number of successful firings of what they called Geophysical Rockets.

One of the largest of their early rockets is reported to have carried a payload of 2,200 kg to a height of 212 km in May 1957. This payload included two dogs that were parachuted back to Earth safely.

Then, five months later, the Soviet Union achieved a great "first" when, on 4 October 1957, they announced they had succeeded in launching into Earth-orbit the world's first artificial satellite. Called Sputnik 1, this weighed an amazing 83 kg. Sputnik 2 was launched into orbit soon afterwards, on 3 November 1957. Not only did it weigh an astounding 500 kg, it carried the first living creature into Earth-orbit, the dog Laika.

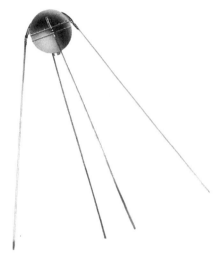

Above: Sputnik 1, the world's first artificial satellite, which remained in orbit until 4 January 1958.

Right: Laika's kennel (1) is seen from the outside, and diagrams (2) and (3) show its internal layout. It contained a food store, air conditioner, receptacles for liquid and solid waste, and instruments to record her pulse, breathing, blood pressure, and the temperature and pressure in her kennel.

For eight days Laika circled the Earth, apparently in good condition. Then, on 11 November 1957, she was painlessly put to sleep for, at that time, no one had attained the technical knowledge of how to recover a spacecraft from Earth-orbit.

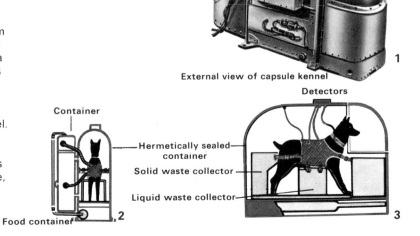

External view of capsule kennel

Detectors

Container

Hermetically sealed container

Solid waste collector

Liquid waste collector

Food container

1

2

3

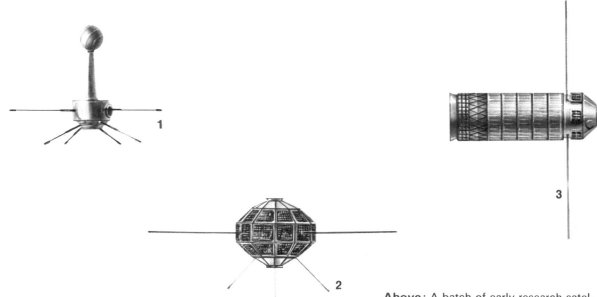

Above: A batch of early research satellites which includes (1) Explorer 10 which probed magnetic fields in space. (2) the Canadian Alouette used radio signals to explore the ionosphere. (3) Explorer 13 which studied micro-meteoroids – small particles of matter travelling through space.

BEGINNINGS OF SPACE EXPLORATION

Although the successes of the Russian scientists had caused the Americans to feel great disappointment they were, nevertheless, the first to applaud Soviet achievements. That America had not won the race to put a satellite into orbit is explained by the fact that much earlier success in producing a small nuclear warhead had meant that she did not have to develop huge booster rockets to give these weapons long range.

Russia, on the other hand, had nuclear warheads that were so large and heavy they needed huge rockets to carry them.

In the long run America's technique of miniaturization was to lead to many important discoveries. For example, data transmitted back to Earth from Sputnik 2 had suggested there was little danger to be feared from cosmic rays – those coming from outer space – or solar rays radiated from the Sun.

However, Explorer 1, a tiny satellite weighing only 8 kg, had a completely different story to tell. It was placed into orbit by a modified Jupiter-C rocket on 31 January 1958 – the first U.S. satellite to enter orbit. When travelling almost 2,500 km from Earth, special tubes to measure radiation, known as Geiger tubes, suddenly went out of action.

The man who had put them on Explorer, Dr James Van Allen, decided they had been choked by very intense radiation, a fact confirmed later by Explorer 4.

Above: Telstar, which provided the very first transatlantic TV pictures.

Above: Russia's Molniya communications satellite.

Modern examples, in synchronous orbit 35,888 km from Earth, stay in a fixed spot above its surface.

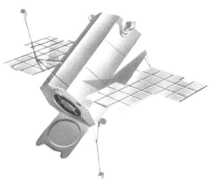

Above: An Orbiting Astronomical Observatory (OAO) which carries a telescope way above Earth's atmosphere for more accurate observation of distant stars.

SATELLITES TO HELP MANKIND

As launch vehicles and launch techniques became more reliable, scientists exploring space were able to send quite odd-looking satellites into orbit to learn about conditions that exist beyond the protective screen of our atmosphere.

Simple spheres began to sprout aerials that could give accurate data measurements, or had panels of solar cells to collect the light from the sun and convert it into energy to power the satellite's batteries.

All this research seemed to make little difference to people like you and I. What did make us sit up and take notice was the satellite Telstar, which first relayed live television pictures across the Atlantic Ocean. It suddenly became possible for us to sit in the comfort of our own homes and watch events as they were happening thousands of kilometres away.

Above: Early Bird, first commercial communications satellite, is famous for many reasons. It enabled millions of people to see the launch and recovery of a Gemini spacecraft, allowed a medical diagnosis when patient and doctor were 6,400 km apart, and let New York art collectors take part in an auction of pictures and books in London. It even made possible the arrest of a Canadian gangster.

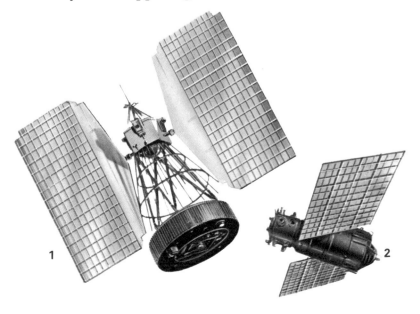

Left: (1) America's Nimbus and (2) Russia's Cosmos 144 are both examples of meteorological satellites.

Many people have suggested that it was unkind to use animals in this way, but since there was every chance the animals would be recovered safe and unharmed this was hardly fair comment. There would certainly have been an outcry against the whole manned space programme if men had died in orbit for lack of proper knowledge.

Now, with successful launch and recovery of dogs in Russia and monkeys in America, man had learned enough to launch himself into space.

ANIMALS INTO SPACE

Although men had been working for years to make rockets that would one day carry them way beyond our atmosphere, they did not really know whether the human body could survive there. Much had been discovered by research rockets, but it needed more than this to make sure that man could travel and live in space.

As early as 1951 the Russians had developed a special cabin that they could attach to the nose of their geophysical rockets. Equipped to maintain a suitable cabin pressure and temperature, provided with air to breathe and chemicals to absorb water vapour and carbon dioxide, it could be separated from the launch rocket at its maximum altitude and parachuted back to Earth.

They chose dogs to serve as the first space voyagers, travelling to heights of 450 km. After landing, they showed every sign of good spirits and a hearty appetite.

In America, events followed a similar pattern, but they chose to use small monkeys of the Rhesus family as their first space passengers. When they had progressed to the stage of being able to put a spacecraft into orbit, their first space traveller was a chimpanzee named Enos.

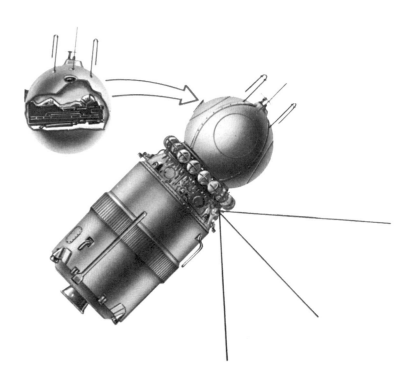

MEN INTO SPACE

THE FIRST SPACEMAN

Shortly after nine o'clock on the morning of 12 April 1961, a twenty-seven year old Russian, Major Yuri Alekseyevich Gagarin had set out on a voyage that recorded his name forever in history.

Told simply, he had been launched in a spacecraft named Vostok 1, to make one complete orbit of the Earth before landing safely 1 hour 48 minutes later, about 9·6 km from the calculated touch-down point.

Throughout the whole world the news of this great achievement was received with excitement. In the U.S. there was also disappointment that the Russians had beaten them to this historic "first".

When Russia announced this breath-taking event, they stated only that the spacecraft weighed 4,725 kg and that it consisted of the cosmonaut's capsule, with landing system, and a separate section carrying the instrumentation and retro-rocket. A retro-rocket is one which is fired to slow the space vehicle for a special manoeuvre, or as it begins re-entry into the Earth's atmosphere.

Above: The Vostok launcher — a massive rocket more than 37·8 m high with a take off thrust of over 453·590 kg.

Left: Gagarin's spacecraft, which was first shown to the public at the Soviet Economic Achievement Exhibition in Moscow in April 1965. The two main components are shown. The capsule containing the cosmonaut's cabin was a simple sphere 2·3 m in diameter. The complete unit measured 7·35 m in length, excluding the aerials.

Right: A cut-away view of Gagarin's cabin. He lay in an ejection seat which also housed his spacesuit ventilation system.

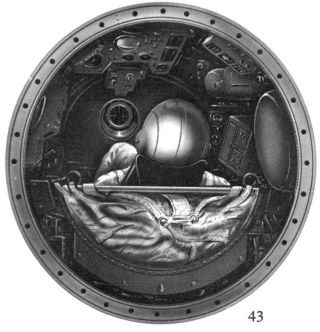

AMERICAN ASTRONAUTS IN SPACE

It was only natural that NASA and its team of astronauts should feel some disappointment that the Russians had achieved the first orbital flight. Wisely, NASA did not allow anyone to make them speed up their planned man-in-space programme.

So it was not until 5 May 1961 that Cdr Alan B. Shepard became the first American to travel in space when his Mercury spacecraft, Freedom 7, was launched in a sub-orbital flight down the Atlantic Missile Range from Cape Canaveral (now Cape Kennedy).

A modified Redstone rocket was the launch vehicle, accelerating to a maximum speed of 8,207

Right: Atlas thunders into the sky at the start of America's first manned orbital flight. The spacecraft is perched on top of the rocket and carries on its nose a tower structure housing a rocket to pull it clear of the booster if an emergency develops at launch.

Above: The Mercury spacecraft Freedom 7 is carried into the air by a modified Redstone rocket on 5 May 1961. This, America's first sub-orbital mission, was an integral part of NASA's cautious approach to putting a man into space.

This caution was often criticised by those who considered that national prestige was of more importance than safety. NASA was not to be diverted from its programme, however, and this methodical approach, testing each step carefully before passing on to the next, ensured that all six Mercury spacecraft, and the ten Geminis which followed, were all recovered safely.

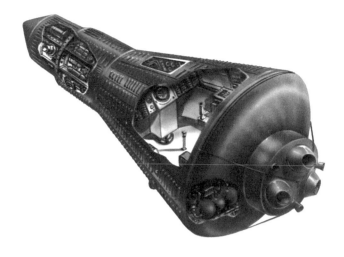

km/h and a height of 185 km before the Freedom 7 capsule was dropped gently in the sea by parachute, 486 km from its take-off point. On 21 July 1961, Capt Virgil I. Grissom made a similar flight in the Mercury capsule Liberty Bell 7.

A more powerful booster than Redstone was needed to put a Mercury capsule into Earth-orbit. Atlas was the choosen booster, but in a test firing on 25 April 1961 the rocket failed to enter its planned flight path and had to be destroyed in the air. Clearly, more testing was necessary before attempting a manned orbital flight.

Tests carried out on 13 September and 29 November 1961 proved successful and, at last, tension mounted as NASA prepared for the most important space-launch that America had attempted.

The date, an important one in American history, was 20 February 1962 – the chosen astronaut a red-haired 40 year-old Lt-Col of the U.S. Marine Corps named John Glenn.

At last came the moment of the final count-down. Atlas, poised on a thundering sheet of flame, seemed to hang almost motionless until, at last, very slowly it climbed and then accelerated away into space. It proved to be an almost perfect three-orbit mission. Almost, because the automatic control system went wrong prior to re-entry and Glenn had to take over the task of firing the retro-rocket himself. In fact, the knowledge that the capsule could be controlled manually proved to be a good thing, for it tended to increase rather than lessen the astronauts' confidence in their craft.

Right: First to "walk" in space was Lt-Col Aleksei Leonov who, together with Col Pavel Belyayev, was launched from the Soviet cosmodrome at Baikonur in the two-man Voskhod 2 spacecraft on 18 March 1965.

Voskhod 2 was fitted with an air-lock, a separate compartment that could be depressurized without affecting the whole of the spacecraft.

Leonov "walked" in space for ten minutes, linked to Voskhod by a 5m-long tether. He operated a TV camera that was fixed to the outside of his craft, and even tried a head-over-heels antic to see if it would make him giddy.

When his "space-walk" was over he re-entered the air-lock compartment, which was jettisoned from Voskhod 2 after he returned to the main cabin.

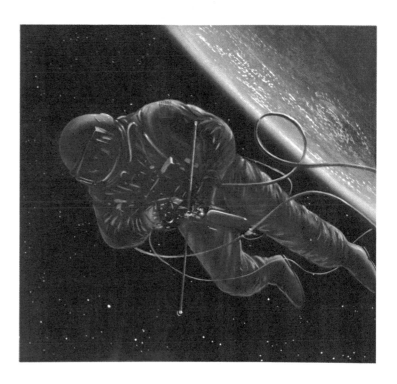

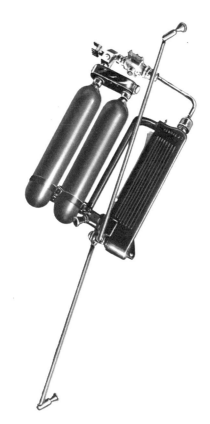

Above: A hand-held unit used by U.S. astronauts to move about when "walking" in space. This particular model has three small rocket motors which are powered by hydrazine and water.

SPACE-TWINS OF TWO NATIONS

Before discussing the very successful Gemini programme, it seems fitting to tell you first about Russia's equally successful Vostok programme which was completed before the first unmanned Gemini was sent into orbit.

You will remember that Vostok 1 had carried Yuri Gagarin on the world's first manned flight in 1961. Vostok 2 was launched four months later, on 6 August 1961, and carried cosmonaut Herman Titov for the first day-long space flight, during which he completed seventeen orbits of the Earth. The longer duration of this flight enabled Titov to carry out a work programme that allowed Soviet scientists to judge the general condition and work capacity of a man in space.

Vostoks 3 and 4 were launched on 11 and 12 August 1962 and made the longest flights up to that time. Adrian Nikolayev in Vostok 3 completed 64 orbits and Pavel Popovitch in Vostok 4 made 48 orbits. The launch of Vostok 4 was very accurate, placing it in orbit only 6 km from Vostok 3. Nikolayev and Popovitch were able to talk to each other and their control centre by means of a continuous radio link.

Vostok 5, launched on 14 June 1963, and piloted by Valery Bykovsky, was joined in space 45 hours later by Vostok 6, carrying the world's first woman cosmonaut, Valentina Tereshkova, who completed 48 orbits. Bykovsky accomplished 81 orbits and 119 hours in space before landing, a record he held for two years.

The Gemini programme, named after the twin stars Castor and Pollux, started, strangely enough, after the Apollo programme that was intended to put men on the Moon.

It was considered that the task of landing on the Moon would be so difficult that it would be wise to start another programme to study the techniques that would be needed if Apollo was to be successful.

Accordingly, the Gemini programme was started, but it was not until 8 April 1964 that a modified Titan 2 ICBM carried the unmanned Gemini 1 into orbit. An array of instruments checked that all was working well, and it burned out on re-entry, as planned, four days later.

On 23 March 1965 the first manned flight of Gemini got under way, when Virgil Grissom and John Young entered orbit in Gemini 3. The most important aspect of this flight was that the astronauts were able to manoeuvre in space for the first time by means of small attitude-control rocket motors fitted to the spacecraft.

Gemini 4, launched on 3 June 1965, carried Edward White and James McDivitt, and was notable for the "space-walk" of 21 minutes carried out by White. Gemini 4 had no air-lock, which meant that before White could leave the craft it had to be depressurized. It was a moment of real adventure, for no one knew for certain that both men could survive in space with only the protection of their spacesuits.

All went well and White, connected to Gemini only by a thin line that supplied oxygen and electricity, floated in space. Gemini 4 landed safely after 64 orbits.

Below: Gemini 6 and 7 travel together in space, some 160 or more kilometres above the Earth's surface.

Rendezvous was not merely a stunt for men to prove they could control accurately their new vehicles in the vastness of space. For America, it was an essential part of their Apollo programme. It was equally important to the Russians but for different reasons. They believed that an Earth-orbiting space station was the best place from which to start out on space exploration. It needed space-walks and rendezvous to build them.

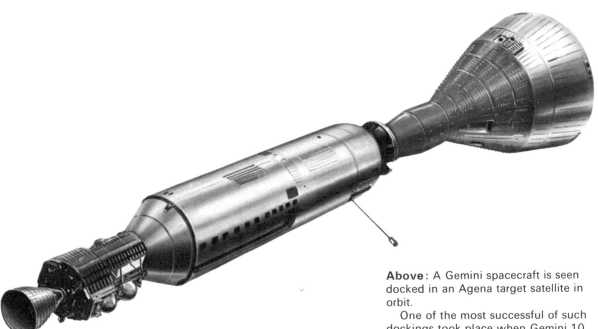

EIGHT-DAY MOON FLIGHT TEST

The programme for Gemini 5 was more ambitious, craft and crew being required to stay in orbit for eight days, the time needed for a journey to the Moon and back. For the first time, fuel cells were needed to supply electric power, as batteries would not last for the eight-day mission. In the event Gordon Cooper and Charles Conrad successfully returned to Earth after eight days in space.

The next launch carried Frank Borman and James Lovell aloft in Gemini 7, on 4 December 1965, at the beginning of what was to be the longest flight then attempted. Eleven days later, on 15 December, Gemini 6 was blasted off from Cape Kennedy, carrying Walter Schirra and Thomas Stafford, their mission to rendezvous with Gemini 7 in Earth-orbit.

This historic meeting, the first-ever true rendezvous between two manned spaceships, lasted for almost 4 hours. During this period Geminis 6 and 7 manoeuvred around each other and photographs taken by Stafford give dramatic proof of the two spacecraft accompanying each other in space. At one stage they were separated by a distance of only 30 cm.

Gemini 6 landed on 16 December, but it was two days later before Borman and Lovell came back to Earth after an absence of fourteen days.

Above: A Gemini spacecraft is seen docked in an Agena target satellite in orbit.

One of the most successful of such dockings took place when Gemini 10, launched on 18 July 1966, with astronauts Michael Collins and John Young aboard, rendezvoused with the Agena 10 target five hours after launch and completed the docking operation successfully fifty minutes later.

The astronauts then fired the Agena's engine for fourteen seconds to carry them to a record altitude of 763 km.

The Gemini 6 and 7 missions had proved so successful that NASA could see no reason for delaying any longer the important docking experiment of two spacecraft in orbit. So an Agena target was launched, followed shortly after by Gemini 8 with Neil Armstrong and David Scott on board. On 16 March 1966, $3\frac{1}{2}$ hours after launch, Armstrong and Scott sighted the target and began to manoeuvre for docking. This took some time but eventually Gemini nosed into the Agena docking collar, which locked on to it.

This was a great "first", but satisfaction was short-lived because very soon afterwards a stabilizer motor on the Gemini jammed in the open position and began spinning the united spacecraft faster and faster. They seemed to be completely out of control, but as soon as Armstrong and Scott understood what was happening they were able to switch to emergency control which brought into use other stabilizer motors to slow the rotation so that they could undock. Free once again from the Agena, they made a completely safe landing in the Pacific.

FROM SPINS TO SUCCESS

The mission of Gemini 9 was also something of a disappointment, for the nose fairing of the Augmented Target Docking Adapter, with which Gemini should have docked, failed to open. Splashdown of Gemini 9 was the most accurate to that date, only about 3 km from the U.S. aircraft carrier *Wasp*.

Below: The Russian Cosmos-186 and Cosmos-188 are seen at the moment of achieving the spectacular first fully automatic docking by two spacecraft in orbit.

On 28 October 1967 Cosmos-186 had been launched into an orbit with an apogee (greatest distance from Earth) of 235 km and a perigee (nearest distance to Earth) of 209 km.

During 29 October the orbit of Cosmos-186 was adjusted so that it would pass directly above Cosmos-188 on its launch pad, and after this satellite had also entered orbit successfully, Cosmos-186 began to "home" on it.

The docking was completed quite automatically without, so far as is known, signals or guidance from Earth.

Perhaps, in the course of time, we shall see Russia using variations of this technique to assemble a space station in orbit.

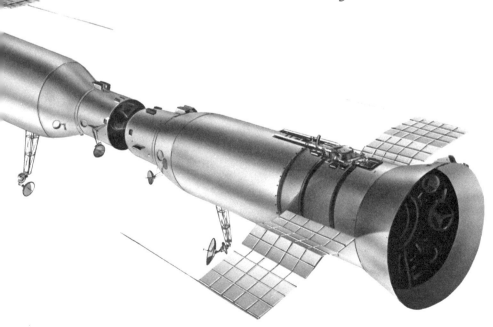

The final launch of the series, that of Gemini 12, took place on 11 November 1966, carying James Lovell and Edwin Aldrin to rendezvous with the Agena target into which they docked successfully. During the mission Aldrin spent more than $5\frac{1}{2}$ hours outside the Gemini craft, proving that by working in short spells with rest periods, men could work in space.

THE FIRST AUTOMATIC DOCKING

From the moment that men first considered voyaging to the Moon, they have argued about the best way to make a flight of fancy become reality.

From the varied arguments evolved two main schools of thought, the Americans preferring the technique they planned to use for their Apollo programme, which is described in detail later in this book.

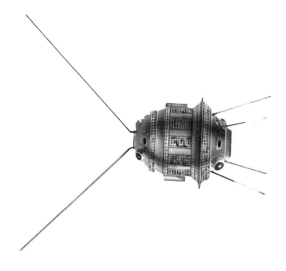

Above: Luna 3 which sent back the first photographs of the Moon's hidden face.

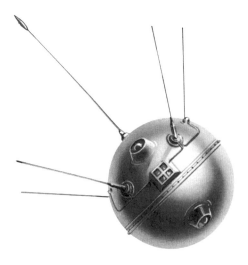

Left: Luna 2 which, on 14 September 1959, became the first man-made object to make contact with another body in space, crashing on the Moon's surface.

The Russians, on the other hand, have favoured the building of space stations in Earth-orbit, from which a spacecraft could take-off directly to the Moon and land there, returning to the space station at a later date. This idea was given striking support when, on 30 October 1967, two of Russia's series of Cosmos satellites, Cosmos-186 and -188, docked together in orbit completely automatically without cosmonauts being on board. They remained as one for $8\frac{1}{2}$ hours until separated by a signal from Earth.

REACHING OUT TO THE MOON

Ranger is shown above a group of Lunar craters. Too much was expected of this spacecraft in its original design configuration. When its mission was reduced to the single task of photographing the Moon's surface as it raced down to a crash-landing, success was immediate and spectacular. Earth-bound telescopes could only study Lunar features some 800 m in width: Ranger's TV camera gave good pictures of craters a metre or so across.

This technique was limited in scope, the pictures originating from a spacecraft approaching the Moon rather than in orbit around it. It was not until the American Lunar Orbiters were launched that almost the entire surface of the Moon was photographed in superb detail.

Very soon after Sputnik 1 had made headlines as the first spacecraft to orbit the Earth, scientists in both America and Russia began to send out lunar probes.

Of course it was a great step into the unknown, and man needed to learn so much about the Moon before he could make any attempt to land on it.

He needed to know if the hidden side of the moon would offer a better landing site, and if the lunar surface was composed of cosmic dust into which a spacecraft would sink and disappear. America started first, on 11 October 1958, launching a rocket called Pioneer 1 which, after travelling 113,780 km, succumbed to gravity and fell back to Earth.

Right: An American Surveyor spacecraft is seen firing its retro-rocket so that it will land gently on the Moon's surface.

As might be expected the method of landing was easy enough in theory, but to control this from a distance of about 386,240 km was no mean achievement. Let us follow, as simply as possible, how this was done.

When Surveyor was about 1,600 km from the Lunar surface a command from Earth caused it to rotate so that its retro-rocket was pointing to the Moon – at the same time the TV camera went into action.

At about 80 km from the surface a radio-altimeter (height measuring device) ordered the retro-rocket to fire and this reduced the craft's speed from some 9,650 km/h to 400 km/h. Surveyor also had three small rocket motors to keep it level and help reduce still more the speed of descent, receiving their instructions from the radio-altimeter and a special speed-judging radar.

Then, finally, about 4 m above the surface, the small rocket motors were shut off and Surveyor landed on the Moon, its shock-absorbers successfully taking the impact.

Russia got within 74,030 km of the target with its Luna 1, launched on 2 January 1959, but this passed beyond the Moon and went into solar orbit, as did Pioneer 4.

Then, on 14 September 1959, came man's first contact with another body in space, when Russia's Luna 2 impacted on the Moon's surface, at some 8,690 km/h, scattering Soviet emblems as it crashed.

PHOTOGRAPHING THE MOON

Less than a month later after Luna 2's success, Russian scientists scored an even greater achievement when Luna 3 passed around the back of the Moon, some 64,400 km above its surface, taking photographs as it did so. These were transmitted back to Earth and provided the first exciting pictures of what the hidden side of the Moon was really like.

America's approach to the problem was a series of Ranger spacecraft, designed originally to take pictures of the Moon's surface, study the composition of its soil and soft-land an instrument package. The first five Rangers were complete failures. Then NASA decided to let Ranger take photographs as it neared the Moon, right up to the moment of impact on its surface. This worked, and Ranger 7 sent back 4,316 exciting photographs before it finally crashed.

The photographs sent back by Ranger 7 were far better than any that had been provided by the most advanced Earth-bound telescopes. Some gave details of craters only a few metres in diameter. Ranger 8 was equally successful. Then NASA decided that the pictures transmitted by Ranger 9, would be relayed on public television circuits. In this way, people throughout the world could share the excitement of a close-up view of the moon's surface.

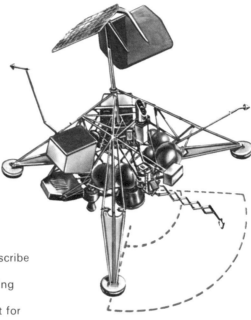

Above: No one could possibly describe Surveyor as beautiful. In fact it is unlikely that a more ungainly-looking craft could have been produced. Nevertheless its design was perfect for the special job it had to do.

The first Surveyors weighed about 997 kg, of which only 27 kg consisted of instruments. Later models weighed more than 1,100 kg and carried 51 kg of equipment. Overall height was 3 m and the feet could be contained within a circle 4·3 m in diameter.

To make sure that Surveyor was not damaged when it fell the final 4 m to the Lunar surface, the three legs were provided with shock-absorbers and the wide landing "shoes" were of crushable material.

Ranger 9 was launched on 21 March 1965, and as it travelled out through space an air of excitement began to spread as millions of people waited for their first view of the cratered and mountainous surface.

Ranger was followed by the even more successful Lunar Orbiters, launched during 1966/67. Not only did they give photographic coverage of almost the entire Moon's surface – a total of more than 36 million km^2 – but produced also the first precise information of the Moon's gravitational field.

ROBOTS ON THE MOON

NASA needed to know much more about the Moon than could be learned from the study of photographs. So, at the same time as they were developing Lunar Orbiter, they started work on a robot explorer named Surveyor which they intended to land gently on the Lunar surface.

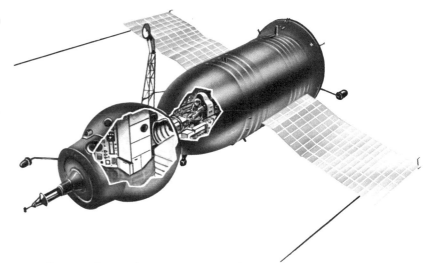

Right: A Russian Soyuz spacecraft which could be more accurately described as a space laboratory, since it is a far more complex structure than earlier vehicles.

Soyuz is designed to allow its occupants to remain in orbit for periods of up to thirty days. This allows a more detailed study than has been possible, so far, of how men will react under prolonged conditions of weightlessness and the strains associated with living and working in conditions that are quite different from those of their natural lives.

Its main task was to confirm the existence of landing areas, able to support a spacecraft; to sample the surface soil and roughly analyse it, and to assess the hazard to be expected from micrometeoroids.

Russian scientists were equally anxious to find answers to the same questions, and on 3 February 1966 Luna 9 made the first successful soft-landing on the Moon in the area known as the Ocean of Storms. Within four minutes of landing, Luna 9's television system began transmitting pictures back to Earth. The TV camera on board made one complete rotation in 1 hour 40 minutes, during which eight photographs were taken from which a panoramic view of the landing area could be reconstructed. Also Luna 9 proved that particular area was capable of supporting a spacecraft.

RUSSIA'S SPACE STATION DEVELOPMENTS

Favouring an approach to the Moon from a space station in Earth-orbit, Russian scientists developed a new series of Soyuz spacecraft.

The first of these, Soyuz 1, launched on 23 April 1967, crashed as it re-entered the Earth's atmosphere,

Right: The complete Apollo spacecraft consists of three units, the Service Module (SM), which can be regarded as its power unit; the Command Module (CM) that carries the astronauts; and the Lunar Module (LM) needed for landing and take-off from the Moon. The picture below shows only the SM, cut away to show a little of its interior. The tank at the bottom, and one above cut-away, contain fuel for the main engine, which sticks out at the left. The fuel tanks are pressurized by helium, stored in the large sphere behind the fuel tanks.

killing cosmonaut Vladimir Komarov. This was the first fatal accident known to have happened during a space flight. Just over a year later Soyuz 2 and 3 were sent into orbit, the latter carrying Georgy Beregovoi.

Soyuz 4, launched on 14 January 1969, and Soyuz 5, launched the following day, successfully completed a most ambitious programme. Soyuz 4 had carried a single cosmonaut at launch, but Soyuz 5 had a crew of three. After rendezvous and docking, two cosmonauts space-walked from Soyuz 5 to Soyuz 4, subsequently landing in that craft; Soyuz 5, with its lone occupant, landed the following day.

Soyuz 6, 7 and 8, were launched on 11, 12 and 13 October 1969 respectively. Their tasks included scientific and technical experiments in space and, in particular, a series of welding tests.

Soyuz 9, launched on 1 June 1970, established a new record of 19 days in space.

MOON LANDING FOR APOLLO

The Apollo programme, which was initiated in July 1960, had three objectives: to place two men on the Moon, to carry out limited exploration of the immediate landing area, and to get the two men, with specimens and photographs, safely back to Earth.

In the first stage of planning, American scientists investigated three ways of getting to the Moon and

back. The first involved a huge rocket to make a direct flight from the Earth to the Moon. The second was known as Earth-Orbit Rendezvous, which allowed the use of a smaller launch rocket but added a lot of complications. The plan finally put into operation was called Lunar-Orbit Rendezvous.

Rendezvous was the key to the entire operation, and you will now understand the vital importance of the Gemini programme and why so much of it was devoted to practising the techniques of rendezvous and docking.

Let us now consider the launch rocket and entire flight plan in some detail.

THE MIGHTY SATURN 5

Development of the rocket known as Saturn began as long ago as 1958. Neither the original Saturn 1 nor the Saturn 1B that followed was powerful enough to place Apollo in Moon-orbit, and Saturn 5, a giant three-stage rocket was built for this task. It was so large that the second stage of Saturn 1B became the third stage of Saturn 5.

At launch Saturn 5 demands no less than 15,240 kg of kerosene and liquid oxygen to lift it off the launch pad. It carries the rocket to a height of about 65 km and a speed of 9,655 km/h within $2\frac{1}{2}$ minutes – then, its fuel consumed, the first stage drops away. The second stage then ignites and races to near orbital speed. As it, too, burns out, the third stage comes to life and burns for about $2\frac{1}{2}$ minutes to provide sufficient speed to place it, and Apollo, in orbit around the Earth.

This is the moment when astronauts and ground control check and re-check every possible item before sending the spacecraft on its journey into deep space.

Left: The wonderful American rocket called Saturn 5, built especially to lift the Apollo spacecraft on its journey to the Moon.
From the base of the rocket project the nozzles of its five Rocketdyne liquid-propellant engines, which have a combined thrust of 3,400,000 kg.
To enable the first stage to carry out its task of lifting the whole assembly to a height of 65 km at a speed of 9,650 km/h, it consumes a total of 2,057,300 litres of fuel in some four and a half minutes.

If all is well, the third stage is then re-ignited for about 6 minutes. When the Apollo modules have attained the required speed, its rocket engines also die and the last stage falls away, leaving Apollo and its crew to travel on alone.

THE LUNAR-ORBIT RENDEZVOUS PLAN

Before Saturn's third stage is disconnected, the three modules that make up Apollo are attached together with the Command Module uppermost, the Service Module in between and the Lunar Module at the rear. The first task – which involves docking techniques – is to change this order into what is known as cruise configuration. This means detaching the LM and docking it to the nose of the combined CM and SM (CSM), thus placing the SM at the rear so that its rocket engine can be used, if needed, for mid-course corrections.

On approach to Lunar-orbit the whole spacecraft is turned so that the SM faces forward and can fire its main engines to slow the spacecraft and put it in Moon-orbit. The next stage involves two astronauts climbing into the LM, which then separates and begins its descent to the Moon's surface. The descent engine is used to slow its speed and cushion its landing on the Moon. Meanwhile, the third astronaut continues to orbit the Moon in the combined CSM.

When the time comes to leave the Lunar surface the LM's ascent engine is fired to blast-off, and lift it back into an orbit where it can dock with the CSM. When this is done, the re-climb stage of the LM is jettisoned. Then, with a fairly long burn of the SM engine, the spacecraft heads out of Lunar-orbit and back to Earth. When final course corrections have been made the SM is jettisoned, leaving only the CM to re-enter the Earth's atmosphere and splash down in the sea.

Above: The Apollo modules shown in cruise configuration. At the top of the picture is the SM, the nozzle of its rocket engine projecting from the rear. The odd-looking LM is shown at the bottom and the cone-shaped section in between SM and LM is the CM, in which the three astronauts are carried.

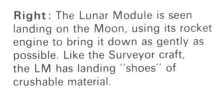

Right: The Lunar Module is seen landing on the Moon, using its rocket engine to bring it down as gently as possible. Like the Surveyor craft, the LM has landing "shoes" of crushable material.

PREPARATIONS FOR THE BIG ADVENTURE

This, then, was the theoretical plan for a Moon landing. But before such an attempt could be made it was necessary to practise the whole technique, omitting only the actual landing on the Moon.

Unmanned launching of dummy Apollo spacecraft had begun on 28 May 1961, and further launchings followed to gain experience. Then, suddenly, tragedy halted the programme temporarily when, on 27 January 1967, astronauts Virgil Grissom, Edward White and Roger Chaffee lost their lives as fire swept through their Apollo capsule during a ground test.

So it was not until 11 October 1968 that Apollo 7 recorded the first American manned space flight since the last of the Geminis had flown in 1966, but it was only an Earth-orbiting test flight.

Just over two months later, on 21 December 1968, Apollo 8 was launched towards the Moon, carrying astronauts Frank Borman, James Lovell and William Anders. NASA was sufficiently confident to let the world watch, by means of television, this first attempt to put Apollo in orbit around our nearest neighbour in space.

So it was that Christmas Eve 1968 became memor-

The diagram below showing the Lunar Orbital Rendezvous (LOR) technique is easy to understand, especially if you read the details given on page 57. It looks more complicated than either of the alternative plans. The first of these involved a direct approach to the Moon by an enormous and costly rocket that would land on and take off from the Lunar surface. The second, known as Earth Orbital Rendezvous, needed two Saturn 5 carriers. Both of these techniques promised to be more costly than LOR, and NASA had to adopt the most economic programme.

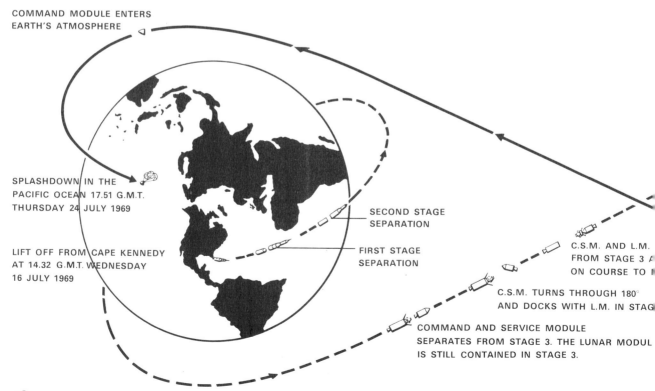

COMMAND MODULE ENTERS EARTH'S ATMOSPHERE

SPLASHDOWN IN THE PACIFIC OCEAN 17.51 G.M.T. THURSDAY 24 JULY 1969

LIFT OFF FROM CAPE KENNEDY AT 14.32 G.M.T. WEDNESDAY 16 JULY 1969

SECOND STAGE SEPARATION

FIRST STAGE SEPARATION

C.S.M. AND L.M. FROM STAGE 3 ON COURSE TO

C.S.M. TURNS THROUGH 180 AND DOCKS WITH L.M. IN STAG

COMMAND AND SERVICE MODULE SEPARATES FROM STAGE 3. THE LUNAR MODUL IS STILL CONTAINED IN STAGE 3.

able for millions of Earth-bound watchers as well as the three men travelling the narrow corridor of space that led to the Moon. Placed in orbit 112 km above the Lunar surface, a rather frightening landscape unrolled slowly beneath Apollo 8. This was one miracle. The other, a sight so wonderful that it could take your breath away, was that of our Earth floating majestically in space.

In March 1969 Apollo 9 had the important task of flight-testing the LM in Earth-orbit, as well as final check-out of the vital rendezvous and docking technique. The stage was now set for the full dress rehearsal and Apollo 10's LM carried Thomas Stafford and Eugene Cernan within 14 km of the Lunar surface – so near and yet so far. How they must have wished that they could make the first historic landing! This was not their task; it was up to them to make sure that, short of the final stage of the theoretical plan – the Moon landing – everything else was as perfect as practice and thought could make it.

Above: After climbing to a suitable height the ascent stage of the LM makes rendezvous with the CM plus SM and docks with them as shown. The two astronauts climb back into the CM and the LM is jettisoned. The LM of Apollo 12 was fired to impact on the Moon's surface.

MEN ON THE MOON

At last the day dawned that had seemed an almost impossible dream. On 16 July 1969 Neil Armstrong, Edwin Aldrin and Michael Collins heard the thunder of their rocket lifting them on the start of the adventure.

Below: At the moment of blast-off from the Moon, we see the ascent stage of the LM as it climbs back into Lunar-orbit, leaving behind it the descent stage which was used for the landing, and also has the important task of acting as the launch platform.

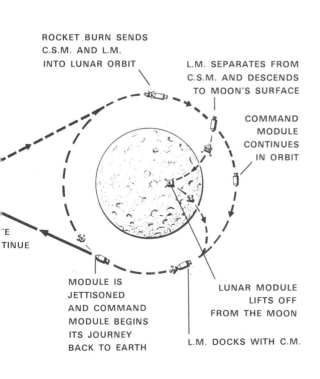

ROCKET BURN SENDS C.S.M. AND L.M. INTO LUNAR ORBIT

L.M. SEPARATES FROM C.S.M. AND DESCENDS TO MOON'S SURFACE

COMMAND MODULE CONTINUES IN ORBIT

'E TINUE

MODULE IS JETTISONED AND COMMAND MODULE BEGINS ITS JOURNEY BACK TO EARTH

LUNAR MODULE LIFTS OFF FROM THE MOON

L.M. DOCKS WITH C.M.

"Moon Walk" illustration shown on previous page.

On 5 February 1971, just over 4½ days after blast-off from the Kennedy Space Centre, Apollo 14's Lunar Module *Antares* made a flawless Moon landing. It carried Capt Alan B. Shepard, USN, and Cmdr Edgar D. Mitchell, USN, to a point only 26·5 m from the designated landing point in the Fra Mauro region of the Moon. Two Moon-walks were planned and, for the first time, the astronauts had a wheeled vehicle to help carry their equipment. Known as MET, standing for Modular Equipment Transporter, it consisted of a neatly-folded rickshaw-like cart, and was soon deployed and loaded. MET was the forerunner of the motorized Lunar Roving Vehicle that was carried on the Apollo 15 mission. It held tools for geological sampling, sample bags, two still cameras, a cine-camera and film magazines.

The first task was the collection of a contingency sample of Lunar material. Shepard and Mitchell set off, the former towing the MET while Mitchell carried the ASLEP (Apollo Lunar Surface Experiments Package). This contained active and passive seismic experiments, a suprathermal ion detector, cold cathode ion gauge and a charged particle Lunar environmental experiment. Additionally, a laser ranging retro-reflector was set up adjacent to the ASLEP site. Later, they carried out a series of seismic experiments to help determine the physical structure and bearing strength of the Lunar surface. A 4 hr 44 min Moon-walk concluded with the collection of about 20 kg of rock samples.

The second period of EVA (Extra Vehicular Activity) was concerned primarily with exploration and sample collection, and the two astronauts travelled about four-fifths of a mile from *Antares*, almost to the rim of Cone Crater. Before *Antares* blasted off the Moon's surface Shepard and Mitchell had collected some 43·5 kg of Lunar material, spent a record 9 hr 25 min exploring its surface — and Alan Shepard, using a makeshift golf club, had made a 366 metre drive!

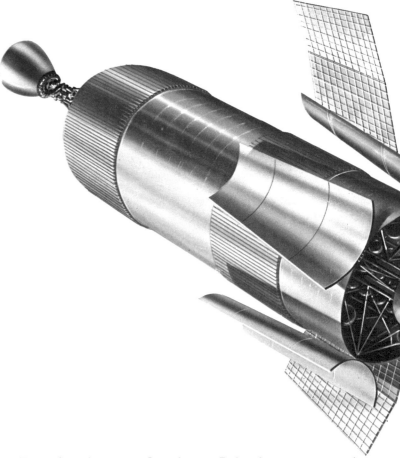

Four days later, on Sunday 20 July, Armstrong and Aldrin clambered from the CM and settled themselves in the LM *Eagle*. After a series of checks *Eagle's* engine was fired and they started their descent to the Moon.

Throughout the world men, women and children were held silent by the drama as TV cameras brought the Moon's surface nearer and nearer. When, just before landing, Armstrong took over manual control to avoid a boulder-strewn area, viewers and astronauts alike were reminded of the danger of the mission.

Seconds later, with Lunar dust clouding the view, *Eagle* settled on the Moon's surface and clearly and dramatically came the words: "Contact lights. O.K., engine stop. Tranquility Base here. The *Eagle* has landed."

And so it was that Americans were the first to land on the Moon. The spaceship from another planet had come to a temporary harbour in the Sea of Tranquility. Even a poet could not have chosen a more suitable name for man's first landing site on the Moon!

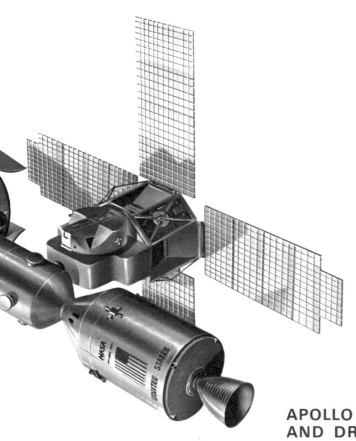

Left: Seen as it would appear in orbit is the Skylab space laboratory. It is a modified Saturn 4B stage, to which has been added an air-lock, a special multiple docking structure and a large telescope.

Before launch the S-4B will be modified and made ready to provide living and working quarters for a crew of three within the vehicle's liquid hydrogen tank, after the contents have been consumed in flight to orbit.

Within the cylinder, partitions will provide separate rooms and handholds, rails and nets will enable the occupants to move around without too much difficulty in conditions of weightlessness, circling some 360 km above the Earth.

APOLLO 12 AND 13 – ACCURACY AND DRAMA

Apollo 11's mission was completed successfully and the CM splashed down on 24 July 1969. Just under four months later, on 14 November, Apollo 12 carried an all-U.S. Navy crew of astronauts Charles Conrad, Alan Bean and Richard Gordon to Moon-orbit, and the LM with Conrad and Bean on board made an extremely accurate landing. The mission was notable for the fact that the astronauts spent almost eight hours on the Lunar surface. The crew returned home safely on 24 November.

It seemed the technique was fool-proof and routine. Apollo 13 proved otherwise, for when it was 331,500 km from Earth, a violent explosion in the SM almost ended the mission in disaster. From that moment on great ingenuity was used by ground controllers and the crew, astronauts James Lovell, Frederick Haise and James Swigert, to bring the stricken spacecraft safely back to Earth. Using the LM as a "lifeboat" they survived the journey, and almost 800 million people watched the end of the drama on their TV sets, as they splashed down safely on 17 April 1970.

THE SHAPE OF THINGS TO COME

LABORATORY IN THE SKY

In order to make the best possible use of the techniques and equipment developed for its Apollo programme, NASA decided long ago to initiate what it called an Apollo Applications Programme.

This name has now been changed to Skylab, and they are concentrating their efforts to put a space laboratory in Earth-orbit towards the end of 1972.

The object of such experiments is to provide a workshop and living accommodation where men could stay for periods of up to 56 days. This would provide knowledge of how they would stand up to the task of living and working in space for prolonged periods. Space flights of comparatively short duration, cannot give scientists sufficient information.

A NEW KIND OF SPACECRAFT

NASA scientists believe that, for some years to come, the most important research will be that which is carried out in Earth-orbit, in craft like the Skylab.

This will mean that men, equipment and supplies will need to be carried from Earth to the orbiting laboratory at regular intervals, and that those who have finished their period of duty will have to be ferried back to Earth.

We know already that such an operation could be carried out by methods that exist, namely by the same techniques that have already put men into and recovered them from orbit. However, the use of

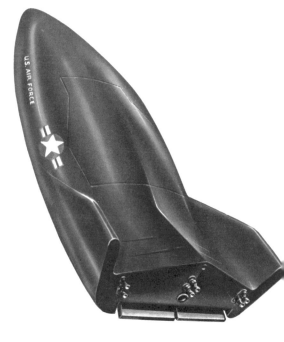

Above: In 1964 four small-scale unmanned lifting-body vehicles were built for flight tests at very high speeds. Known as the SV–5D PRIME (Precision Recovery Including Manoeuvring Entry) they were tested successfully at re-entry speeds of 28,150 km/h.

Left: A typical design study for a future space ferry vehicle. Much thought is being devoted to develop the most suitable vehicle for this important requirement.

The HL-10 was powered originally by an XLR–11 rocket engine, and this was used for initial testing after a period of unpowered gliding flights.

The XLR–11 engine is to be replaced by three hydrogen-peroxide rockets, each of 227 kg. thrust and capable of being fired one at a time, or together, to provide the pilot with varying degrees of thrust. The object of this is to carry out experiments to find out if the space-shuttle vehicles that have been proposed will need engine power for use during landing.

NASA plan also to fit an Agena rocket engine in the HL–10 at some future date.

once-only rockets and re-entry vehicles would cost far too much money for such an idea to be practical.

This started investigation of a completely new vehicle, known as a lifting entry-vehicle or lifting-body. It was designed so that it could travel in space and yet be able to manoeuvre in Earth's atmosphere after re-entry and end its flight by landing more or less like an ordinary aeroplane.

Studies for such vehicles began in 1957, and by 1963 an early unpowered design was towed in to the air and then allowed to glide back to a normal landing. This early vehicle proved to NASA that it was possible for a pilot to fly and land such a craft.

Aircraft of this type have been slowly developing since that time. They were tested initially by carrying them high into the sky beneath large bomber aircraft, where they were released from heights of about 13,000 m and allowed to glide back to Earth.

Rocket engine powered versions of these aircraft are now being flown and it seems likely that development will, in time, provide a suitable vehicle to operate a shuttle service between Earth and orbiting spacecraft.

Below: In Britain, designers had ideas for a rather different vehicle to do the same job.

Known as Mustard (Multi-Unit Space Transport And Recovery Device), it consisted of three manned lifting-bodies launched as a three-component "pack".

The two outside units served as boosters which, soon after launch, would turn away and land. The central unit would continue its flight into orbit and, at a later date, make a return flight to Earth, provided with a heat-shield for protection during re-entry.

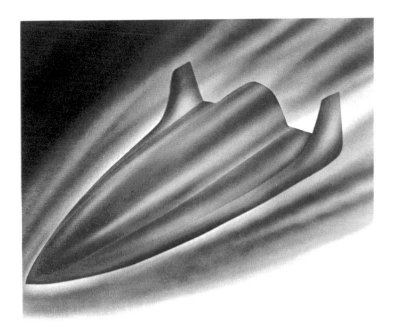

SURVIVAL IN SPACE

Although the task of designing a rocket to get men to the Moon and back was a tremendous job, costing almost unbelievable sums of money, it may come as something of a surprise to know that enormous expenditure has been allocated to perfecting the spacesuit worn by the astronaut.

If you think what this suit has to do, it is not quite so surprising. On the surface of the Moon, for example, it must provide air to breathe and create within the spacesuit a pressure that will enable the astronaut's lungs to operate in the same way they would in Earth's atmosphere. It must have safety devices to pressurize it immediately if, during flight, the spacecraft should suddenly lose its pressure. It must be strong enough not to tear easily, flexible enough to let him move without too much effort, and make provision for him to eat, drink and dispose of the body's waste products. It must also provide insulation against heat and cold, protection against radiation and also be fireproof. No wonder it costs a lot of money!

GOING-PLACES ON THE MOON

Mobility systems for use on the Moon's surface, like the "Pogo" and Jet Flying Belt, obviously have limitations for Lunar exploration. It is easy to see

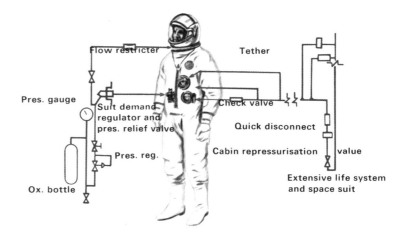

Right: A diagram which gives some idea of the complicated equipment that is an integral part of the spacesuit worn by the astronauts.

Flow restricter

Tether

Pres. gauge

Suit demand regulator and pres. relief valve

Check valve

Quick disconnect

Cabin repressurisation   value

Pres. reg.

Ox. bottle

Extensive life system and space suit

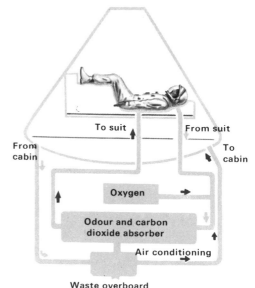

To suit   From suit

From cabin   To cabin

Oxygen

Odour and carbon dioxide absorber

Air conditioning

Waste overboard

that their small size will allow their users to travel only short distances, although this is an improvement on walking.

NASA are interested in the development of vehicles that will allow exploration over far greater areas and have already awarded a contract for the design of a Lunar Flying Vehicle (LFV). It would use as fuel residual propellants from the descent stage of the LM. NASA have stated that such a vehicle must be capable of travelling a minimum distance of 16–24 km.

Suit and cabin temperature indicator

Cabin pressure indicator

Oxygen quantity indicator

Pressure indicator (first stage)

Attitude director indicator

Flight director controller

Pressure indicator (second stage)

Left: The control and instrument panel of a Gemini spacecraft. It looks very complicated, but hours and hours of training made it possible for the astronauts to know their way about it instinctively and to read the vital instruments as quickly as we can tell the time by a glance at our watches.

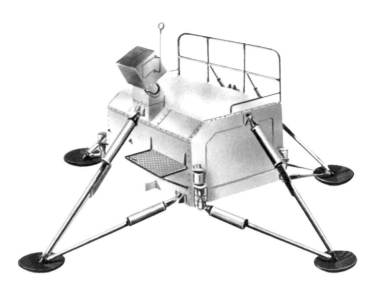

However, vehicles that rely on the power of rocket engines use a great deal of fuel, and to transport this to the Moon is expensive. A vehicle that could travel on the surface, like an ordinary car, would be far less demanding on fuel. It could be made of such a size that it would provide its occupants with protection against wide temperature variations, as well as from radiation and micrometeoroids.

Various designs for what were called Molabs – mobile laboratories – were originated some time ago. Great ingenuity has been used to develop wheel systems that would allow the Molab to climb a vertical rock face 2·13 m in height, and to cross huge cracks in the surface, up to 2·44 m wide. Wheels would have individual electric motor drives, getting their power from a liquid oxygen/liquid hydrogen fuel cell of the type developed for the Apollo spacecraft. NASA awarded the contract for the development of the Lunar Rover Vehicle to the Boeing Company's Aerospace Group in America. Their vehicle was used on the Apollo 15 mission to the Moon.

STARTLING RUSSIAN SUCCESSES

While scientists in the U.S. were considering the projects mentioned above, their counterparts in Russia had prepared a couple of surprises.

On 12 September 1970 Luna 16, an unmanned spacecraft, was launched to the Moon, and on 20 September it made a soft-landing on the Lunar surface. This procedure involved the use of a new type of descent engine that was controlled by an on-board computer.

After a successful landing, automatically operated drills took samples of the Moon's surface from depths down to 35 cm, the material then being transferred to sealed containers. Twenty-four hours after landing Luna 16 took off from the Lunar surface and landed back on Earth on 24 September, complete with its rock samples.

Thus, a completely automatic spacecraft had duplicated a mission similar to that of Apollo 11 and 12, although the Lunar exploration was not so detailed as that carried out by the American astronauts. It was, however, what a NASA spokesman described as "a major engineering and scientific achievement".

People concerned with or interested in space flight had hardly finished discussing this really amazing achievement when, on 17 November 1970, Luna 17 made the second automatic landing on the Moon. This time it carried a Lunokhod 1 remotely-controlled mobile surface vehicle that began short-range exploration of the landing area in the Sea of Rains very soon after touch-down. All over the world scientists were amazed at the brilliance of this exploit.

Below: The upper stage of a launch rocket is seen making a landing on the surface of the Moon.

Such a vehicle, after venting of any surplus propellants, could be quickly and easily converted into a Lunar base, by pushing it lengthwise on the ground.

To protect its occupants against radiation or micrometeoroids, it could be covered over with Lunar soil, but it might be difficult to give adequate insulation to cope with the wide range of temperature between Lunar day and Lunar night.

There seems little doubt, however, that one day Lunar laboratories will serve as research stations where scientists, astronomers and doctors would be able to study the problems of travelling and living in space for long periods.

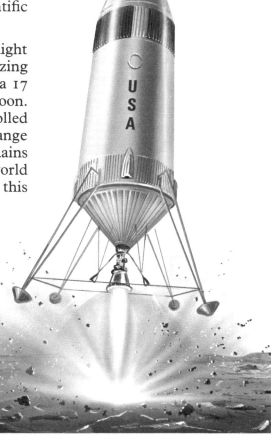

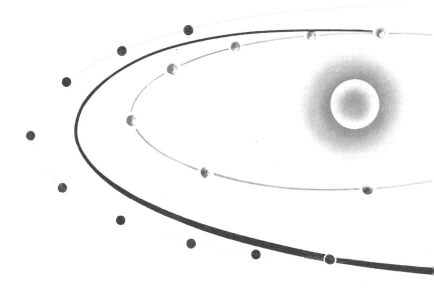

POTENTIAL OF THE
LUNA-LUNOKHOD COMBINATION

Early newspaper pictures suggested that Lunokhod was a strange mixture of vintage car and Victoriana. In fact, it had some resemblance to the Bendix Molab pictured on Page 68, with a similar type of flexible wheel, though the Soviets chose to use eight of them.

Lunokhod 1 was equipped to collect and analyse samples of Lunar soil, radioing its findings back to Earth. It also had a TV camera, sensors to prevent it overturning when under control of an on-board computer, and an ability to be controlled from Earth. A very great technical achievement, it is clear that Luna-type automatic-landing spacecraft plus Lunokhod-like explorers will be extremely useful. They will make it possible for man to find out a great deal more about distant planets, without any need of exposing a human crew to the unknown hazards of travelling for long periods in a state of weightlessness, confined within a small spacecraft.

Below: One of the proposed designs, that of the Lockheed company, is seen in our illustration. This does not really give a true impression of the size of this unit, which would weigh around 203 tonnes.

Intended to be assembled in orbit 511 km above Earth, it would measure 32·8 m in length by 28·6 m wide, and would be built up basically from a series of spheres 5·48 m in diameter and cylinders 9·14 m long and 3·05 m in diameter.

The whole structure would rotate slowly to provide some degree of artificial gravity for its occupants, and power for all essential services would be supplied from a nuclear reactor. In the event of breakdown a small piston engine would give emergency power.

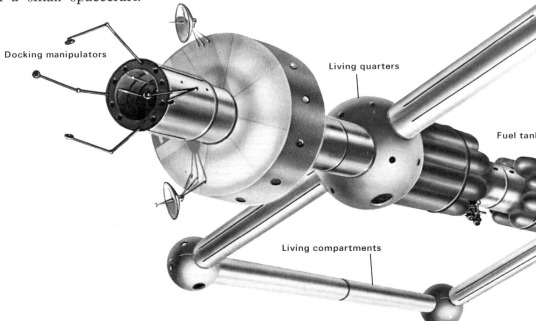

Docking manipulators

Living quarters

Fuel tank

Living compartments

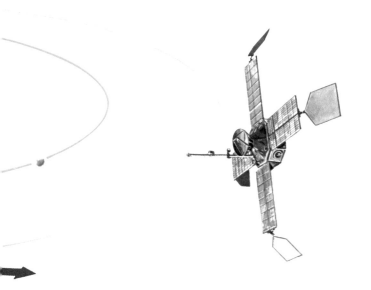

Left: Adjacent to this caption is seen a picture of Mariner 4, first space probe to take and transmit pictures of Mars to excited scientists on Earth.

Very different from the streamlined rocket that started it on its journey, the strange windmill-like object would seem to be incapable of a 217 million kilometre journey. But streamlining is not needed in non-atmospheric space, where even delicate cobweb-like aerials can be extended without suffering any damage.

Above: You can see in the form of a diagram how Mariner 4 was launched from Earth to intercept the planet Mars nearly eight months later.

In our diagram the green line and globes represent the movements of Earth from which Mariner was launched, its course shown by the continuous red line. Mars is shown as the red globe linked by a blue line.

The calculation of a trajectory (a journey between two planets) to make such an interception is very complicated, for not only is the Earth rotating and travelling through space as Mariner is launched, but the target Mars is also following its own orbit at a different speed. To add to the problem the force of the Sun's attraction also deforms the spacecraft's trajectory.

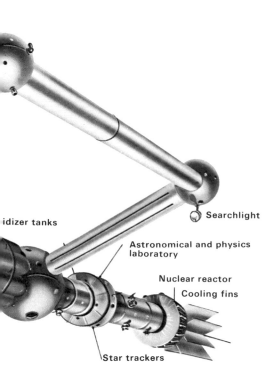

idizer tanks

Searchlight

Astronomical and physics laboratory

Nuclear reactor

Cooling fins

Star trackers

EXPLORATION BEYOND THE MOON

We have seen already that it has now become possible for man to make the three-day journey to the Moon with a fairly high degree of reliability. It is only a matter of time before an Earth-Moon return flight could become routine and reliable, if such journeys have a useful purpose to serve.

At the present stage of the development of space travel, exploration beyond the Moon presents far more difficult problems, not least of which is the time spent in making the journey. Our solar system consists of eight other planets, and at the present stage of spacecraft development it would take about three months to reach the nearest and about $45\frac{1}{2}$ years to reach the most distant.

While this latter figure may seem a long time, it is but a tiny instant in comparison with the time it would take us to make contact with our nearest galaxy, that of Andromeda. Even assuming that we could develop spacecraft able to travel at the speed of light (1,080 million km/h), our world would have aged by four million years before the craft completed the return journey.

LOOKING AT OUR NEAR NEIGHBOURS

It is clear that our present knowledge limits us to the exploration of our nearest planets. In the same way that the V-2 rocket showed the way to a manned Moon landing within 25 years, our early probes to Mars and Venus will almost certainly lead us on to far more advanced vehicles that will let us extend our searching eyes and inquisitive brains.

Already both American and Russian scientists have sent out unmanned probes that have solved some

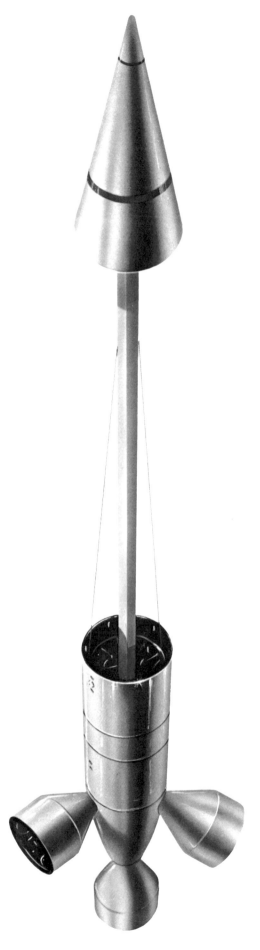

questions that have puzzled astronomers for many years.

America's probes were named Mariners. The first one, launched on 22 July 1962, went off course and was destroyed a few minutes later because it was feared that it might land in the North Atlantic, endangering shipping and human lives.

This was a great disappointment, but Mariner 2 which soared into the sky on 27 August 1962, brought the first new knowledge of planet Venus. After a journey that took 109 days, it passed close enough for its radiometers to detect and record a lot of valuable information. It did not seem that Venus would offer a suitable environment for man and Mariner 5, launched on 14 June 1967, was able to confirm that Venus had a turbulent, stormy atmosphere, was intensely hot and that the planet's "air" was mostly carbon dioxide. It was clear that Venus would be quite inhospitable.

Mars remained our only hope for immediate exploration, for the next nearest planet, Jupiter, would need a journey of nearly three years. America's Mariner 4 passed within about 9,000 km of Mars on 15 July 1965 and the first photographs were sent the 523 million kilometres back to Earth. Their quality was nowhere near as good as the pictures of the Moon that had been transmitted by Ranger, but they enabled scientists to decide there was little hope of finding any trace of life, as we know it, on Mars. This was confirmed by Mariners 6 and 7 that followed in 1969.

RUSSIAN PROBES TO THE PLANETS

It was to be expected that Russian scientists would also be anxious to learn as much as they could about our nearest planets at the earliest possible moment,

Left: A design proposal for a space station that could be used for periods of up to five years. The cone at the top of the picture contains a nuclear generator to provide power.

but trouble with the development of suitable electronic equipment put them far behind the work being done in America. It was not until 1 March 1966 that they achieved what could be regarded as really rewarding results, when their space probe Venus 3 crashed on to the surface of the planet after which it was named.

Venus 4, which followed in 1967, became the first ever probe to soft-land an instrument capsule on another planet, lowered to the Venusian surface by parachute. It transmitted back the information that the planet's temperature varied between 40 and 280°C, and confirmed the Mariner 5 verdict that the atmosphere was almost completely carbon dioxide.

INTO THE FUTURE

What is likely to be the pattern of development in space flight? We can only try and make a fairly intelligent guess. At the moment it would seem that the new techniques demonstrated by Russia's Luna 16 and 17 will make it possible for scientists to explore the remaining planets of our solar system. Beyond that, it would take $4\frac{1}{2}$ light years – $4\frac{1}{2}$ years travelling at the speed of light – to reach the nearest star, Alpha Centauri. This is far beyond our present abilities and will need the development of entirely new propulsion systems. Rockets may even be developed to carry passengers from London to New York so fast that they will have arrived before they have had time to have a snack on board!

Above all, let us hope that co-operation between men of all nations will preserve international peace. May I end by quoting the words engraved on the plaque left on the Moon by Armstrong and Aldrin: "Here men from the planet Earth first set foot upon the Moon, July 1969 A.D. We came in peace for all mankind."

Right: Hyperion, a suggestion for a passenger rocket, travelling from New York to London. Carrying 110 passengers, it would travel at 27,000 km/h.

INDEX